Bob

H.

2013

Love Momma (Mom)

THE RED FOX FATHER

INTENTIONAL ENGAGED INTERACTIVE

DAVID A. PENNEY

CROSSBOOKS
PUBLISHING

CrossBooks™
A Division of LifeWay
1663 Liberty Drive
Bloomington, IN 47403
www.crossbooks.com
Phone: 1-866-879-0502

First published by CrossBooks 05/20/2013

ISBN: 978-1-4627-2739-1 (sc)
ISBN: 978-1-4627-2738-4 (hc)
ISBN: 978-1-4627-2740-7 (e)

Library of Congress Control Number: 2013907778

Printed in the United States of America.

This book is printed on acid-free paper.

Dedicated to my wife, Jody and my children,
Alayna, Matthew, and Jenna.

Special thanks to Raegan Atkinson

Table of Contents

INTRODUCTION

S o one day I am going to work just as I have been doing for the last fifteen years thinking everything is fine. My perspective is such because my supervisor has been telling me that "everything is fine" and "I am happy with your performance." By the end of the day I would discover that he was not the decision maker. That night the carpet was pulled out from under me, and I landed on my proverbial derrière.

I took it like a man, though, and went to the hospital to let my wife know that things were changing a bit. She was a couple months pregnant with our third child and struggling with the pregnancy. I was actually on the verge of hiring a full time nanny to care for my daughter, Alayna, then six, and my son, Matthew, then four. After careful analysis of the situation I realized that a world of opportunity was out there; I had no career to risk losing. As I am sure you have experienced, sometimes our great careers are the very things that we won't risk losing to achieve bigger things. Later that night, I told my wife that I wanted to use my newfound "free" time to do something special, to do the things that I never had time to do. I never thought that I was particularly talented at anything, but then she informed me, "David, you are a great father." I loved hearing her say that because I take great pride in being a daddy and realize how blessed I am. I respect the position God has granted me, all the more so because I have a friend that can't have children of his own, and I know how hard that is for him.

It was at this point I set out to write a book, the very book that resides in your hands. I did this because being a dad is more than just passing on my genetic code or creating somebody to help harvest the crops. My own father left my home when I was eight years old. I remember that little guy, me, standing in the formal living room on the green shag carpet in front of my parents, who were on the couch, (it had an orange and green paisley pattern, which I know seems like a terrible match, but it worked in 1976). My brother was to my left, two years older and my best friend. My uncle and aunt were in the room as well, my uncle on the right and my aunt on the left, no doubt there to try to counsel my dad to change his mind. They couldn't, and he didn't. I remember my father running through the situation. "Boys," he said, "I don't love your mother anymore. We are getting a divorce." At eight years old, I didn't quite understand what divorce was, but my brother asked, and we were subsequently informed, "Mommy and Daddy are not going to live together anymore."

Not realizing all the ramifications that would proceed over the next thirteen years, I knew enough to cry my eyes out that day. Part of my childhood was kidnapped; I was crushed. I spent the next ten to twelve years of my life with my newfound identity: "child of a broken home." Although my dad kept in contact, it wasn't the same. He had been my idol, my leader, my mentor, but when things fell apart between my mom and him, my brother and I were caught in the crossfire of the vicious war that ensued. Friendly fire or collateral damage, whatever you call it, it hurt the same. There weren't that many assets, but the legal battles were not finalized until I was about twenty-one years old. Yep, thirteen long years later. I now see that eight-year old little boy as a different person than the man I have become. My heart goes out to him and to the millions of other little boys and girls out there today whose fathers are less than what the job requires. Having the determination of a heartbroken eight-year old little boy, I knew very early in my life that I was going to become the best dad who ever walked the planet. I look at this responsibility as a mission from God. I strive to achieve proactive parenting, being intentional about my instruction, engaged in their lives, and interactive in their play.

Enclosed are my thoughts, ideas, wisdom and stories that share my objective of becoming, a Red Fox Father. I hope you find them beneficial because you owe that eight-year old little boy or girl, or whomever you have created, your best.

WHY THE RED FOX?

When I first found myself as a floundering father, I took an inventory of what it takes to be a good father; no, I mean the best father. So I turned where everybody turns for factual information and landed on the internet. There I found that the red fox had been awarded the number one father in the animal kingdom by the National Wildlife Federation. This made me curious. I wanted to understand just what the National Wildlife Federation thought made a good dad. Here is an excerpt from their analysis:

> *Researchers have seen fox dads exhibiting much excitement about their pups, playing with them endlessly. One father was even observed waiting for a watchful aunt to fall asleep and then quietly calling to his pups to come play with him.*

http://www.nwf.org/news-and-magazines/national-wildlife/
animals/archives/1996/a-fathers-day-top-ten-animal-fathers.aspx

It was the word "endlessly" that caught my attention because that is just what being a good father is all about: endlessness. The red fox father teaches his pups how to forage for food by collecting the food and burying it for the pups to find. He sets up his kids for success, and it is based on this success that the father makes certain they can move from the den. Finally, the red fox is loyal to his mate and feeds the whole family while his mate takes care of the young pups. There have been no official observations of the red fox father doing any of these things begrudgingly.

Based on this information I coined the term Red Fox Father and decided to define what it meant to be a great dad. I landed on three qualities; being intentional with my instruction, interactive in my children's play, and engaged in their life.

To be intentional is to have a purpose. When it comes to your parenting are you doing it on purpose or merely responding to needs, wants, and desires?

Interactive is easy. Do you play with your children or do you watch them play? Dad, if you are a bystander in your children's playtime you are not only making a huge mistake you are missing out on a great part of life. I have hidden behind the luggage in the hall closet more than one time for a game of hide and seek. Get interactive.

Engage is to hold one's attention. It amazes me when I see young children with new fathers the children want to engage with their father but the child can't hold their father's attention. Once the child becomes a teenager the father wants to engage and then wonders why he can't hold the teenager's attention. Weird huh? Be engaged from the beginning and stay engaged throughout.

Dad, it only takes three things to be a Red Fox Father, intentional, interactive, and engaged. It's that easy. So let's get started and be the number one father in the animal kingdom, the Red Fox Father.

Do you have Strategery?

One night on *Saturday Night Live* Will Ferrell did a skit on George Bush and used the term "Strategery." This was an attempt to make fun of how President Bush stumbles over words. The Bush Administration thought that it was so funny they actually adopted the term and began having meetings and calling them "Strategery Meetings". So my question for you is, do you have a strategergy?

I have heard fathers say, "if I can only get my boy to eighteen years old alive," or "I just want to get my daughter to eighteen without getting pregnant." Seems as if the standards have been lowered quite a bit. Okay, I must admit, there have been times in my fatherhood period when I have felt the exact same thing, thinking that success would be measured by just getting my children to eighteen without any major mistakes. However, when I calm down and think more clearly, I realize that most likely within the five to seven years *after* my children turn eighteen they will make two of the most important life decisions they will ever encounter: 1) they will choose the person with whom they will spend the rest of their lives, and 2) they will decide what they are going to do for a living. Most likely they will make these decisions while not living under my wing.

After I consider this, getting my children to eighteen with such shallow goals is not in their, nor in my best interest. Many fathers think, I will provide food, clothing, and education and that is my job. However, the flaw in this thinking is that a father has only approximately eighteen years to prepare his children for roughly seventy years of living. You need a strategy. At work, I do not implement any new process without a strategy for success. I never negotiate any deals without first thinking through a strategy. I never counsel an employee on his or her performance without a strategy. So why, when it comes to something as important as raising my children, do I find myself without a strategy? The most important assignment God has ever given me, and I have no plan, no direction, and no strategy? I have lowered my goals to "just keeping them alive"! Heck, I don't even go to the grocery store without some sort of plan, but when my kids are four or five years old I have already capitulated?

Not me my Red Fox followers. I have created a strategy. I am going to formulate a plan. What am I creating? I want my son to be more than just alive at eighteen and my daughter more than just not pregnant. The first thing to do is to elevate my goals, write them down, put them on a timetable, and implement the strategy. Victory will be mine, and my children will be ready for the tough "life decisions" they will have to face. I have been on a mission, my friends. If you don't have a strategery, get one!

The Mission Statement

My mission is to be the type of father who represents the Love of God to my children, who builds in them confidence, teaches them to respect and act respectably, and demonstrates the value of wisdom and in making wise decisions. I want to teach them to love others and to not take advantage, nor be taken advantage of.

My mission is to be the type of husband I would want my daughter to marry and my son to be. I want to relay to them the benefits of being loving, joyful, peaceful, and patient and how to exercise kindness, gentleness, and self-control, all the while balancing these qualities with the ability to be strong enough to thrive in a tough world.

My mission is to discipline with love, instruct with patience, and guide with purpose, keeping the end in mind, that of creating a wise, confident, kind adult who is in a growing relationship with his or her Creator and Savior.

I will achieve this prayerfully, being intentional about my instruction, engaged in my children's lives, and interactive in their play.

This is my mission, a Mission from God.

Be intentional, be engaged, be interactive. Be a Red Fox Father.

OVERDRAWN

I used to hear my wife say, "It feels like all I do is yell at the kids all day long." I would then look at her as if she were completely crazy because, when I came home from work, the children were usually well behaved and happy. I naturally assumed that I was just the perfect father, and that she just allowed herself to be stressed. Anyway, when I would arrive home the kids were happy. It wasn't until I stayed home all day for a period of time that I realized that the kids were not always happy; they tended to get a little used to you. They got tired of listening to your every command and the excitement wore off a little bit, actually, a great deal.

Unfortunately, I let the cat out of the bag one night, and in a weak moment I told my wife, "It feels like all I do is yell at the kids all day long." She then looked at me as if I were completely sane. "Ah ha, now you know what it feels like when you are not the big exciting news returning from being gone all day. They got a little used to you, didn't they?" They did indeed.

At this point, I had a couple of problems, one of which was that my wife was apparently not completely crazy at all. Were there other things about which she was actually sane? Are vegetables really good for you? Do I need to really wash my hands before eating? Should I really put the toilet seat down? Oh my gosh, do I need to listen better??? Who knew where this could lead? Oh, the anarchy this could cause!

More importantly was the second problem: were my feelings correct? Did my children go to bed and think, "Geez, all Daddy did was yell at me all day"? What a heartbreaker. I guessed that if I felt like all I did was yell, they most likely thought all they got was yelling. This had to change.

The next day I opted for a different approach. What would the Red Fox Father do? I meant the animal, the Red Fox. The Red Fox constantly teaches his pups how to stalk prey, hunt, and hide from danger. The Red Fox plays games with the pups to give them the skills to survive in a tough world. Throughout this process the Red Fox celebrates even the simplest things that a young pup accomplishes. I realized that when my four year old took off his shirt without help, I took it for granted; after all, I had been doing this a couple of times each day for thirty seven long years. I began celebrating some of the more "ordinary" things that my children accomplished, careful not to overdo it. I don't want my children to think that every little thing they do requires some great response of praise but I did celebrate when they were able to do something that is usually difficult for a child at that stage of life. Stuff I had previously expected. I didn't lower my standards; I just allowed my children a little glory in some of the little things that previously I would have just expected them to perform without comment. I didn't overdo the praise, at times it was just a simple comment, "you did good."

Simply put, I made deposits in their little emotional bank accounts. Prior to this, I was overdrawn. Surely we all have read the leadership

THE RED FOX FATHER

books about how you must make deposits in your employee's or spouse's emotional bank account in order to make withdrawals, but I had never applied it to my children. (Heck, I'm not even sure I had applied it to my spouse, but that is another book, one perhaps called *The Seahorse Husband* because the seahorse male bears the young.) I had been bouncing checks all over the house, and at the end of the day, I was getting a notice from the Bank of Subconscious: I was Overdrawn. So with no government bailout to be found, I needed to implement change.

When I implemented this new praise deposit procedure, I found that the number of reprimanding withdrawals I had to make were fewer. I had reestablished peace with my children.

Now I think that the thing to remember here is that many small deposits work better than one large one. You can't make withdrawals all day long and then expect at night to make a huge deposit and not get contacted from the Bank of Subconscious; you are going to get a notice. Don't lower your standards; just recognize that little extra effort with a little extra deposit, such as saying "good job". Recently my son came home from school, took off his shoes, and left them in the middle of the floor. A few moments later, without my saying a word, he picked them up and put them where they belong. Deposit: "Nice work son."

One more observation to mention: when you only make withdrawals the contrast between withdrawal and nothing is only half that between a deposit and withdrawal. The withdrawals become much more important when compared to a deposit than when compared to nothing. In other words, I have found that I have been able to reduce the amount of withdrawals as well as the frequency.

There's more to say on this topic, but I need to wash my hands before dinner. We're having vegetables. Maybe she is not crazy after all.

Be intentional, be engaged, be interactive. Be a Red Fox Father.

CHOOSE YOUR BATTLES

George Custer died at thirty-six years old. I personally think that his legacy is tainted for people that don't know history. Actually, George Custer was a very successful military leader during the Civil War. He and his troops played a decisive role in ending the Civil War, and he was present for General Lee's surrender. I can't imagine that a failed military leader would have been invited to such an event, but there he was. Most of us only know Colonel George Custer for leading all 256 troops into Little Big Horn for total annihilation in what is commonly referred to as Custer's Last Stand. After the Civil War George was courted for several jobs, and some even wanted him to run for Senate, but he eventually turned all his opportunities down and reenlisted. I feel certain that if Custer had known that his men were about to face over 1,800 Native Americans at Little Big Horn, he would have reconsidered advancing as he was significantly outnumbered. Custer was actually known for doing his homework, checking the battlefield, evaluating his enemies, and determining the best line of attack. Custer usually chose his battles wisely. In the summer of 1876, Custer and his troops were destroyed by the Souix Indians and Crazy Horse; history tells us that Custer chose this battle.

I am sure that any military general will tell you that the most important aspect in winning a war is to choose your battles wisely. Not just their location but also their timing. If location is important, and timing is everything, then the key to winning is making certain that you choose your battles wisely. I completely agree with this strategy when it comes to military battles, and I will even go so as far to endorse that strategy in business negotiations.

Recently I was discussing with an acquaintance of mine children's wants and needs. I specifically explained to this parent something that I was not allowing my children to take part in after which I was moderately reprimanded for being too strict, I was told, "Ya know, you have to choose your battles." I immediately bought in. *Yeah, that's a good strategy. Choose my battles.* But then I took time to consider something very important: I am not fighting a war! My children are not some foreign enemy trying to take over my land and rule the people. Although it feels that way sometimes, this is not the reality. My children are merely trying to expand their circle of influence. The way I see it, I am their leader, and I am leading my family, my troops, if you will, and in my army, what my wife and I say goes. Now, keep in mind that my children are young, so why, at this point should I not choose every opportunity to lead? Aren't my children so important to me that I should choose every battle? Especially since I know I can win every battle. You can bet your beret! Allowing children to make important decisions without proper guidance is what leads them down a road filled with regret, and the real battle is lost.

Now, I realize that when my daughter is sixteen I will in fact have to use wisdom to decide when to get involved in providing strict guidance and when to loosen up. I don't think that I live in some vacuum that is going to exempt me from discussing dress code with my daughter. I do believe that if I don't choose all the battles when she is seven, I won't be able to choose any battles when she is sixteen. So fast forward nine years, and my daughter wants to wear Daisy Dukes to school. Battle chosen, battle won. My hope is at this point she remembers that throughout her life I have been her leader, not her enemy.

Red Fox Fathers, keep in mind that your job is to lead your children and your family. I would suggest that before one can win the battle, one needs to clearly define just who or what your enemy is. It is not your children, not your wife. You are not at war with them. There is a war going on, though, and you are the general. You are leading your troops to war! You may disagree from time to time as to the proper strategy, but until your children make a rank that qualifies, their input should be considered optional. I listen to my daughter, let her know that I understand her wants and needs, and then literally tell her, "I will take under advisement." As with any group of people that has a leader, you will have dissent sometimes. It is wise to consider other options, but do not be afraid to just say no. It is important to choose your battles, but it is also important to know thy enemy. So don't put your children in a place to be just that, it is not their intent. Your children are just trying to stretch their wings to be ready to leave the nest. Just make sure that when they do, there is no Crazy Horse lurking.

Red Fox Father's if you choose to battle your children, you are not being smart about choosing your battles, you are being ignorant about choosing your enemies and one day all too soon, your last stand may be with your teenager in your own home and at this point, your significantly outnumbered.

Be intentional, be engaged, be interactive. Be a Red Fox Father.

TICKETMASTER

I remember a job whereby we got free tickets to just about every event brought to the Atlanta area. This was the year I attended numerous plays including *Phantom, Rent, Stomp,* and *Tap Dogs.* We also went to the MLB All-Star Game, the Homerun Derby, and, yes, the Superbowl and the World Series. In addition to these events, I also went to countless MLB baseball games, NFL games, monster truck shows, and even the circus. There was nothing quite as nice as the owner of the business giving me a stack of tickets and allowing me to distribute them as I saw fit. Even though I signed every paycheck at that particular business, when I received those tickets, I was more important. I was, in fact, the king of the world because there is nothing quite as nice as a free ticket. Heck, the President of the United States didn't hold as much power as I had back then. Like most good things, they come to an end . . . until I had children.

I had a friend ask me the other day how I was teaching my six year old daughter about money. My answer was that I wasn't. Not only was I not, I had not even considered it. She would beg for stuff in a store and I would say "yea" or "nay." I never thought to use her greed to actually teach her something; the whole concept was fascinating. Over the next couple of days, and with my employment status at the time, when my daughter asked for toys, dining out, entertainment, etc., I decided my friend was right: it was time to teach her about money. (It was then I realized that my wife could use the same education.) Of course, the allowance was the first discussion that we embarked on, (not for the wife, for the children), and I have to tell you, I was not real excited about giving money away for just living. This reminded me too much of welfare and my hope was that my children one day would understand that people "reap what they sow." That doesn't really seem to apply anymore in today's society, but I at least wanted to make it apply in my home. Understanding that the whole welfare-for-children thing didn't excite me, my wife came up with the following solution.

The Ticketmaster. She created a system whereby the children could earn tickets (the power just makes me shiver all over again). Each Sunday, each child would receive ten tickets for the week. Behavior above the call of duty could earn tickets, and poor behavior required a ticket to be paid back. Then on the next Sunday we would cash out each ticket for a quarter and issue another ten tickets. A couple of rules would exist: the children would not be allowed to ask for a ticket (this could actually cost them a ticket) and at the end of each week a portion of their earnings had to be saved and a portion given away. At the end of each week, the children could do whatever they wanted with the leftover money. One good part about this plan was that my wife and I didn't feel guilty at this point about the junk the kids bought. It was their money, their decision. On a side note, the first week we implemented it my daughter gave me her money back, knowing my unemployed status. (I guess the plan worked!)

The whole goal for Ticketmaster is to teach children that doing good is standard, being great earns, and acting poorly costs. In our household when things start getting out of hand all I have to do is mention revoking a ticket, and a warm blanket of calm obedience ensues. I have also noticed that when a child goes over the top with considerate, good behavior, the ticket is a powerful tool. Instant reward, instant punishment. I really think that whoever invented the spanking needs to take a look at this. Apparently greed is substantially more powerful than pain. *I should have known this already.* A word of caution: it took my children a good week and a half before they completely understood the concept. The full rewards of money management have not yet been attained, but I can see the wheels spinning. I saw my daughter stand in Target and actually begin to look at the prices and the cost versus benefit concept. *I wish the wife would do this!* It is fun to watch a six-year-old weigh a Hannah Montana toy versus Polly Pockets. Oh, the quandary! Bottom line, I can highly recommend Ticketmaster to teach children how the world used to work, when a hard day's work was the criteria for earning. Also, it is an excellent tool to begin understanding saving, giving, and spending wisely. Who knows, maybe I will start charging an exorbitant handling fee! I genuinely feel as if I am making progress with the children on the whole money earning/management concept. If only I could do the same with the wife.

Be intentional, be engaged, be interactive. Be a Red Fox Father.

THE CROWN ROOM

There is no place on earth like the Atlanta airport. I have been there often and I am one of those type people that doesn't like busy places and this place seems to be the busiest. I think the Magic Kingdom at Walt Disney World can be fairly busy but it is a relaxed busy, not a business busy. People are not as rushed. Nearly everybody on the planet has been through the Atlanta airport and those that haven't apparently will have a connector flight there as they pass from this life into heaven, it's that busy.

I used to have Crown Room privileges. The Crown Room was a place that I could escape from all this input. It had a living room setting, wall to wall carpet, refreshments, and clean bathrooms. When I went to the Atlanta airport I could feel the life being sucked right out of me because it was so busy people flash in and out of your life in seconds. As tens of thousands of people were trying to get on place to the other I felt years fall away from my life and then I would enter the Crown Room, take a deep breath and try to recover. The Atlanta airport was simply too much input for me. It was overwhelming and the Crown Room was my escape from it all.

Consider all the input our children get compared to what we got when we grew up. At my house growing up we had three television stations and one was PBS. I got an Atari at a garage sale after some other family was bored with it and had moved onto Nintendo. The Atari had a couple games. Games like Pong where a white ball bounced back and forth between two paddles. If this doesn't sound bad enough, I have no recollection of any other games that we had because they were worse than Pong. When we left the house there were no electronics unless you called flashlights electronics. Oh yeah, of course there was no internet. The input my parents had to compete with was limited and could easily be removed or I from it as these items were not available remotely. Back in the 70's and 80's we all had a "Crown Room", an escape from the input.

Now consider our children. The number of television stations is infinite. I currently have more Spanish stations than total stations that I had as a child. ESPN has more sports only channels than I had total channels as a child. The point that I am making here is we now have lots of input. In addition to the infinite number of television stations I have made available video games galore. If the input doesn't come via the Xbox then it is the Wii. If it is not the input from Xbox and Wii then the input comes from Facebook, Twitter, or other places on the endless internet, all brought to you by way of a smart phone. Endless amounts of input with the ability to access it from nearly anywhere at any time. Who knows what input our children receive. It's like they are in the middle of the Atlanta airport and input has the ability to flash in and out of your child's life in seconds. Before you can see it coming it's already gone and as parents we have no idea it was ever there. Our children get too much input, too accessible, coming too fast and all this can be in the palm of their hand. It is quite a lot for a child to decipher and way too much for them to oversee.

Red Fox Fathers our parents did not have to compete with all this outside input. Our children get input overload. Three television stations and an Atari are not that much to compete with. You, however, have endless amounts of input to compete with and its everywhere you go. We all know that questionable wisdom and guidance come from these areas of input. Simply put, Red Fox Father, **you cannot be your father's type of father and expect to be successful**. I am not saying that your father didn't do what was required to raise a well-adjusted young man but if you expect to duplicate the effort and input and get the same results your dad got you are making a terrible mistake. You are getting out inputted from multiple sources and your children are being guided by these unknown sources of information. Red Fox Fathers have two choices; either reduce the input from all this technology or increase the input coming from you. I recommend both.

Dad, you need a Crown Room; a place or time for you and your children to be able to escape from foreign influences of input. Ever wonder where bad language or poor behavior comes from? Check your sources, it could be the input passing through and you had no idea it was coming and no idea it was ever there. Put your children in the Crown Room for a while and get in there with them. No electronics, no games, no television, and no internet. Don't feel bad when you remove these devices and input from your children. I know first-hand that children don't enjoy the Crown Room as much as I did in Atlanta. My children have spent a great deal of time in the Crown Room and we pull out a board game or a puzzle. Remember these things? Games where a child has to count, figure, strategize, and be creative. You might even find yourself in a real conversation. There is nothing like putting together a 1000 piece puzzle with a young teenager to make her whole world visible to you again. See what you just did there? Removed foreign, unknown sources of input and put your child in a position where you get increased input. This of course means that you have to be able to break away from your smart phone also. Remove the technology sources of input and insert your years of vast wisdom and knowledge. The Crown Room is that easy.

Red Fox Fathers, you would never leave your child wondering around in the Atlanta airport with tens of thousands of people swiftly passing in and out of their lives, why allow the same in your home? We now live in an age where a sexual deviant middle-aged man from Russia could have communication and influence with a twelve-year-old girl growing up in Normal, Illinois all with the click of a button and you would never know. Get in the Crown Room, monitor the activity closely, and take some time to reduce the input. When you read your child's texts, email, or internet browsing history and they say you are spying on them feel free to say, "you're absolutely right I am." When my children are outside I keep an eye on them. When they go over somebody's house, I know who is there. When they go to the movies, I know which one they are watching. Why would I not monitor who they communicate with over the internet and what they are viewing?

For the sake of consistency here, don't hesitate to protect your children in their cyber world. It's more dangerous than your neighborhood.

Be intentional be engaged, be interactive. Be a Red Fox Father.

SMACKDOWN AT THE HILTON

When you walked into the hotel room, you just knew that an egregious crime had been committed there. One mattress was dangling between the floor and the box spring; the other had slid off the bed and into the wall. The bedding was all over the place, a lamp fallen down, the pillows were strewn everywhere, and the phone receiver hung from the bedside table. Anybody would have guessed that the room had been tossed, and, at a minimum, a theft attempted.

In this particular case an egregious crime had not been committed, but there was an attempted theft. I actually personally stopped a crime in progress. At forty-two years old, six-foot-two, 178 pounds, I was able to singlehandedly foil a theft in progress. I was so proud of myself I would like to tell the full story here.

My wife wanted to return to Atlanta to enjoy its vast shopping and restaurants, and we were able to get a hotel that had a living room and two bedrooms. On one side of the suite was the master bedroom with a bath, and on the other side was a room with the aforementioned two double beds. Usually when my family is on vacation, while my wife is getting ready for the day, I enjoy standing about three feet behind her for those two hours and

21

constantly repeating, "hurry up," "let's go," "we're late." It just seems to start the day off right and get her attitude straight for the day. Also, I honestly believe that it might actually shave a few seconds off her get-ready time so we can get in line at some store's cash register faster.

On this particular day, I'm not sure why, I was a little relaxed and decided to forgo the normal get-ready ritual. This day my five-year-old son and I were in the room with the double beds with about eight pillows strewn around. Now I don't know about you, but in my world eight pillows + hotel room + five-year-old-boy = pillow fight. I would think that every father knows this equation. So my son was immediately blindsided by a pillow to the back of the head. He then did what any little boy would: he armed himself and took his rightful position on one of the beds. What ensued was far beyond a pillow fight, (dare I call it a pillow war) but strictly conventional at this point. For thirty minutes I ducked, dodged, and dived pillows, gathering up my weaponry and returning fire, my son giggling non-stop during the entire conflict. I quickly realized that I can heave a pillow so hard that I can knock a five-year-old boy clear off his feet. At times, when out of ammo, hand-to-hand combat was the only solution, my son buried in pillows or pinned in between the mattress and the wall giggling uncontrollably. Later I would learn that this little event completely made my son's day.

It was then that my wife walked into the room, at the same time that I was winding up the long distance artillery from the opposite corner and she witnessed the pillow screaming across the room, impaling my son in the back, and his falling on the mattress that lay half off the bed. It was at this point, that an attempt was made to steal something, my sons masculinity. "David!" she declared. "You are going to hurt him, and you are teaching him bad things!" Red Fox Fathers, I respect my wife, love her dearly, and generally listen to her. Not this time. While she knows how to heal boo boos, make a mean mac and cheese, teach reading and math, and an expert at making the house a home, I find her ill equipped to harness, direct, and facilitate the masculinity that comes standard with each little boy created. I took some time and listened to her demands, and then I did what any normal father should do . . . reload.

There have been many times when I have had to ask my wife not to emasculate my son, not to deprive him of power or virility. Afterall, a boy should be allowed to still be a boy. Fathers, life is hard, and while your wife can show your son where his dirty laundry goes, it is up to you to show him how to get his clothes a little dirty sometimes. While your wife can lovingly and delicately kiss boo boos and apply band aids ever so perfectly, it is up to you to teach your son the value of "walking it off" because this world offers fewer band aids and more opportunity to have to walk something off. You, and only you, have the power to take what God has generously allowed you to have, a son, and make him what God intends for him to be, a man.

Don't think for a minute that your son doesn't need you. He does, and he will never be too young or too old for a couple metaphorical pillow fights. I can tell you from experience as a little boy who was raised almost exclusively by a woman, it is in your wife's nature to mother. Women come by it naturally, and thank God they do, but too much mothering, and you end up with a little boy who becomes a man without the traits and understanding of just what manhood is all about. Now I know that one pillow fight isn't enough of a lesson to toughen up my little guy; however, a steady dose of "Dad time" is just what the boy needs. I would submit to you that if your wife doesn't get a little upset with you from time to time because you are playing too rough, breaking a couple of household items, or just simply being a guy with your son, then you are not fathering enough. Get in the game, Dad. It is time to push the envelope a bit and do what I did; take an opportunity to reload. Opportunities for pillow fights only last so long.

Go ahead, Dad, make his day.

Be intentional, be engaged, be interactive. Be a Red Fox Father.

LIFE COACH

There was a time when I was "in between jobs." That is a nice way of putting it; unemployed is more descriptive. I tried on "retired" for a while but when I used that term, people just thought that I was super successful, and I didn't want to lead people horribly astray. Whatever you call it, I spent a great deal of time at home, and it didn't pay very well. So, that being the situation, I took up a new career, one I was extremely excited about. I became a Life Coach. At the time I had two clients with a third very interested, expecting to sign in June. In order to prepare for my new career I did an extensive amount of research on Life Coaching, and I was anticipating the payoff to be substantial. The best part was that my clients were great people and equally excited about the opportunity. They were fairly successful at their stage of life, and my goal was to merely supplement their current success. All of them were very good at what they did, but still had untapped potential.

For those of you that don't know, Life Coaching is the process of teaching people a certain set of skills or direct them in obtaining certain goals. I think my personal goal for my clients follows the US Army motto; I want my clients to "Be All You Can Be". I honestly believe that helping my clients obtain their full potential will be the most rewarding part of the entire job, although I am looking forward to that, my intention is to also bask in the process of getting there. This is a trip whereby getting there is going to be as good as the arrival. The funny thing about my "new" venture is that it is not really been that new. I have been Life Coaching for about six years, I was just too busy to realize it. I was too busy providing for my family, but what the heck was I providing? Sure I was providing food, shelter, and massive amounts of toys, but I think that I was not providing the necessities; principles, responsibility, and massive amounts of wisdom.

Although I should keep my clients identity confidential by now you most likely know who they are, my soon to be six year old daughter, my four year old son, and the baby that is being born in June, I am a Life Coach, I bet you are too. What services are you providing your clients? Just food, shelter, and a massive amount of toys or do you get down to the necessities? I think that my job description as Father I allowed to be defined by modern society, to provide stuff, so I am redefining my job description, Life Coach.

Your job doesn't end at five pm, it begins; and the payoff is going to be substantial.

Be intentional, be engaged, be interactive. Be a Red Fox Father.

The Castle

It was designed with a beautiful princess in mind and exuded the majesty, wealth, and nobility of the king. Although the construction was ongoing, the front of the castle was nearing completion. As you came up the wide, flat, and winding road, you were greeted by a huge arch just before the bridge. On either side of the arch were small gate houses that were the starting point for a huge wall around the circumference. If an enemy were able to scale the wall, the other side dropped straight down into the moat, which was filled with bright blue water and whose sides were perfectly straight, placing the exterior wall of the castle in a defensible position. The castle walls were thick and each stone designed specifically for that particular spot in the wall. The base of the castle was huge, undoubtedly for the peasants to safely engage in market-type activities, but for the royalty there were five towers and a whole entire second level reserved for those of nobility and related servants. From the ground to the second level there were huge staircases that formed half circles, each staircase starting at the base of the wall and extending clear up to the towers. Each tower was placed for a heavenly view of the nearby ocean and beach. It was quite a sight to behold.

Christopher was drawn to the ongoing construction. He was a preoccupied young man when his eye first caught the enormous structure. He watched from a distance as the construction was happening, but as things went on, he knew that he wanted to be able to say, "I helped build that." As time went on, Christopher volunteered his own time to participate in the construction. Christopher was very young and had zero castle construction experience, but the other carpenters were quick to allow him to help even though he did more destruction than construction at first. The foreman knew that Christopher needed this in his life. At this time in history, young men like Christopher learned how to earn a living from their father. However, Christopher's dad did not teach him this particular type of construction; in fact we will never learn if his dad taught him anything. The foreman on this job knew Christopher's dad was nowhere to be found, so he let him use this castle as on-the-job training. The foreman showed Christopher how to build a wall, create a staircase, carve out windows, dig a moat, and all the other items that went along with creating a castle. Truth be known, the foreman felt somewhat sorry for Christopher because the foreman had been in a similar situation in his younger days. So there they were, creating a castle together, side by side, with the sun on their backs, sweat dripping from their noses, and onlookers watching each step in amazement as the entire building came together. Christopher and the foreman bonded for the brief period they had together, but after the castle was completed, they parted ways, forever. Nevertheless, they took the memory with them.

This castle was not in France, nor could it be found in England. Actually, this castle no longer exists because before the foreman, another construction worker, and young Christopher parted ways, they destroyed the castle, and no sign of it remains to this day.

This castle was constructed in Destin, Florida, made of sand by me, my son, and some other father's son named Christopher. Some other father who thought that improving his golf game was more important than spending time with his son, Christopher. My son and I took a raw piece of beach and began excavation, digging a moat and building a road. It was then I noticed a seven-year-old little boy on the beach alone with his mother, drawn to the bucket of shovels and mass of sand we were moving. In no time, I had a volunteer, and with nothing more than, "My name is Christopher. Can I help?" we began major construction. I later learned that Christopher's dad was missing out on teaching his son how to create a sand castle. I also think his dad was missing out on creating a relationship, creating a memory. We spent about three hours digging, designing, crafting, watering, and carving out sand to eventually take turns stomping said castle into smithereens. I noticed other little boys checking in occasionally, noticing the improvement, and I also noticed other fathers glued to the latest novel or sports magazine.

Red Fox Fathers, there will be a day when my son doesn't want to build a sandcastle with me when we go to the beach. But not this day; it was mine and so was he. There will be a day when little Christopher doesn't want to build a sandcastle with his father, either, but it wasn't this particular day. But his dad was golfing and now had one less opportunity to build a sandcastle, one less opportunity to build a relationship, one less opportunity to build a memory. You see, I have no doubt that Christopher remembers the three hours he spent sweating in the hot sun, covered in sand on the beach in Destin with two strangers. I also know that Christopher's dad did not get any better at golf that day. So, dad, go enjoy that golf game, your book, or your sports magazine because at the end of the day you may know a little more trivia about sports, or be able to sink that fifteen-foot putt. But I will be on the beach, with my son and maybe yours, creating more than a sandcastle.

Be engaged, be interactive, be intentional. Be a Red Fox Father before you have one less opportunity.

UNEMPLOYMENT 101

A friend of mine called me and said, "Guess what? I am unemployed. Now what?" I had mixed emotions. I didn't feel like I should be a source for how to handle unemployment. However, at the time I did have four solid months of experience at unemployment, and I did believe that I "did unemployment" about as well as anybody. So whereas this book is about being a father, this particular chapter is about how to be an unemployed father. I hope that you will never need this sage advice, but if at some point you find yourself holding this prestigious position in life, maybe you can reflect on my vast knowledge and experience and push through.

First and foremost, your wife is not the reason that you were laid off, nor is she going to be able to comfort you in any way, so don't expect it. Imagine if you were a stay-at-home dad and the only source of income was your wife and she was laid off. You haven't worked in years, your spouse is out of work, your financial security and welfare just took a huge blow, and it is all entirely outside of your control, in somebody else's hands. Ouch! At least your layoff is under your control; your wife right now is entirely relying on you, so allow her some grieving time. Don't look to her to be your source of strength. You need to be a leader in the face of this trial, so put on a positive front.

Plan for the long term. Live like you are going to be unemployed for a very long time. I mean this spending money and also with your time. Don't say things like, "I can't start that project because I will be employed soon," or "I am not going to start working out because I will just stop when I get employed". It ain't going to happen. Make a plan and work it.

Exercise often. Not only does this relieve stress, it will help you feel better about yourself, and it keeps you busy. One of the most important things is to avoid the television. Set up a routine, do what you always wanted to do, lay out some goals. I highly recommend sports that you can do by yourself. It will be difficult to schedule a tennis match at 10 am during a weekday because most of your friends will be at work, but 10 am is a perfect time to jog around the lake jamming with your ipod.

If your wife hasn't made a "to do" list, make your own. For some of us, within minutes of unemployment we are blessed with a "to do" list from the wife. At first you will want to ceremoniously burn it by the stove, but consider this: these things need to be done and ironically enough, you have the time. I started with the cheapest ones first: I painted our bedroom for $50, fixed all kinds of things for cheap, hung some pictures, stained the deck for another $50, used all the gift cards we had laying around, went through everything in storage, completed some yard work, and cleaned out the garage. Again, stay away from the TV.

Find out what being a housewife is all about. My wife happened to be on bed rest and pregnant during my unemployment and not doing her job was not an option. I allowed her a leave of absence under the Family Medical Leave Act of 1993 and became interim Mom. Do it for real, too, not just parts of it. Take over the complete job description. When you learn what your wife does all day, you will look at the whole stay-at-home thing completely differently. Not only will it let you know how easy your job was, it will also help motivate you to find a job . . . fast.

Some don'ts.

Don't look for a job for eight hours a day, this will just flatten your self-esteem and it is not going to help anyway. I do recommend a daily search and continual networking, but to spend the entire day doing this is a recipe for disaster.

Don't watch TV! I made the mistake at lunch one day watching Sports Center. With my stomach full, the TV on, I thought that I would just take it easy one day. The TV made its way over to Jerry Springer. There I found myself fully in a trance. Apparently Joe was dating Melissa, but also intimate with Melissa's brother. Joe said that he was just drunk and was not gay, but Melissa's brother said, "You sure do get drunk a lot because we have been together a lot." Joe, again denied he was gay. Melissa was considering taking Joe back; after all, he was just the victim of random gayness. To prove that Joe was not gay, he decided to inform Melissa that he was also intimate with her best friend, and, thankfully, Melissa's best friend was a woman. "See, I ain't gay!" Of course, Melissa's friend Sharon was in love with Joe and wanted him back, so then Melissa had to start a fight with Sharon while Joe and Melissa's brother watched. The equally disturbed audience was into the entire thing. There I was with remote in hand and an hour of my life completely gone forever. Jerry did do a nice job of wrapping it up with some words I know we could all use: "If you are in a relationship, it is best to not get drunk and have sex with your girlfriend's brother, and if you do, then don't try to prove that you are not gay by cheating with your girlfriend's friend." Oh, the wisdom. There, I have just wasted some of your time, too. Don't turn the TV on.

Finally, and I think most importantly, do allow yourself to mourn. Losing a job is like losing a friend that was there every day, and love it or hate it, you most likely find yourself completely surprised by the loss. Allow yourself to be upset, sad, or even angry, should the need arise. The last thing you need to do is be mad at yourself for being mad about the situation. You have taken an unexpected loss, so allow the sulk. Just don't stay there, or it will annihilate you. Interval depression is all right for a period, so let yourself visit, but don't unpack your bags and stay. If you do, it will come out in the interviews.

By using your unemployment wisely it is my hope you will be able to look back on what is going to be a very short period of your life and know that you took advantage of the position that you found yourself in through no fault of your own. You could very well look at this as an opportunity to rediscover what your goals are, and, maybe you will even write a book!

Be intentional, be engaged, be interactive. Be a Red Fox Father.

You Can't Handle the Truth!

I was talking to a friend of mine the other day, and he was telling me how God is to blame for a bad thing that happened in his life. I tried to relay that sometimes things just happen, that people make bad decisions, and that life is tough, but that God is not always to blame. I got nowhere, so I decided to concede that God is truly to blame, if he would concede that God is all powerful and all knowing.

With his permission I would like to tell you his story. My friend's name is Alan. Alan is about my age, early forties/late thirties, and is married with two children, a daughter, six, and a son who is four. His beautiful wife was pregnant with their third child when this story takes place. By all measures you would consider Alan successful. He had a good career, making a good living, and being promoted to a place of prominence with over six-hundred employees in his employ.

Early on a cool November morning Alan was having to face a decision. His wife was struggling with the pregnancy and had to be hospitalized. The doctor had said that when Alan's wife was released, she would be bedridden for at least six months. Alan had a decision to make, quit his career and stay home to take care of his wife and kids or hire a nanny. Well, surely all of us would agree that the best course of action would be to simply hire a nanny and not quit what it took Alan fifteen years to create, a great career. So Alan went about his due diligence, securing interviews, references, background checks, drug tests, all the usual when hiring for such an important role as nanny. Alan found the perfect fit, a responsible, mature, and experienced nanny, and went back to work knowing everything at home was taken care of.

Then it happened; the worse. The nanny was driving the kids to school one day when a truck t-boned the minivan. The van flipped numerous times and settled in the median, bent metal, broken glass, bodies strewn. Alan's life flipped over, too. The daughter didn't survive the accident, dead at the age of six, the four-year old son wouldn't be playing baseball that night or ever again, paralyzed from the neck down. A couple months later the third baby was born, but it wasn't the same. Alan harbored bitterness towards the baby because he felt if his wife hadn't been sick because of the pregnancy, none of this would have happened. Alan's wife just couldn't handle it all. She had to be committed to protect herself, from herself. This was when I got a call from Alan. "Why, God, why?", he asked. "Why didn't God intervene? Where was he?"

Where was He indeed?

Consider this alternate story, if you will.

With his permission I would like to tell you the story of a friend of mine named Alan. Alan is about my age, early forties/late thirties, and is married with two children, a daughter, six, and a son who is four. His beautiful wife was pregnant with their third child when this story takes place. By all measures you would consider Alan successful. He had a good career, making a good living, and being promoted to a place of prominence with over six-hundred employees in his employ.

Early on a cool November morning Alan was having to face a decision. His wife was struggling with the pregnancy and had to be hospitalized. The doctor had said that when Alan's wife was released, she would be bedridden for at least six months. Alan had a decision to make: quit his career and stay home to take care of his wife and kids or hire a nanny. Well, surely all of us would agree that the best course of action would be to simply hire a nanny. Or would it? But then it happened; the worse, Alan was laid off from his career, a devastating blow. The economy was the worst Alan had ever seen in his lifetime, and his particular industry was going belly up. This is when I got a call from Alan. "Why God, why?" he asked. "Why didn't God intervene? Where was he?"

Where was He indeed?

You see, Alan never hired the nanny, the car accident never happened, the daughter did not die, the boy is still playing baseball, and his wife is fine. But Alan didn't know what didn't happen. He never knew what "would be"; he only knows what he thinks "should be".

Alan, like us, was apparently too focused on what "should be". Only an all-powerful, all-knowing God knows what "would be." Alan should have been able to keep his career, but God knew there was more at stake. I would presume that what "would be" is not ever dependent on what we think "should be". Because God is all-powerful and all-knowing, maybe, just maybe, God did intervene when Alan got laid off because the "would be" was far more worse than what is.

Imagine the movie *A Few Good Men*, consider God, played by Jack Nicholson, and Alan, the attorney, played by Tom Cruise.

Alan: Did you order the lay off?
God: I did what I had to do.
Alan: Did you order the lay off?
God: Alan, you want answers.
Alan: I think I am entitled.
God: You want answers!
Alan: I want the truth!
God: You can't handle the truth! Son, we live in a world where we have walls, and those walls have to be guarded. I have a greater responsibility than you can possibly fathom. You weep for your job loss, and you direct anger and blame at me. You have that luxury. You have the luxury of not knowing what I know, that your job loss, while tragic, saved you a much greater loss. My action, while incomprehensible to you, saves you a great pain. You don't want the truth because if I revealed how close you were to greater loss, you would live your life paralyzed by fear forever. Son, you want me on that wall, you need me on that wall, and I have neither the time nor inclination to explain myself to a man who rises and sleeps under the very blanket of free will and salvation that I provide and then questions the manner in which I provide it. I would rather you just say thank you and went on your way.
Alan: Did you order the lay off?
God: You're absolutely right I did.

Come on, be honest, a lot of us blame God for something. We all do. After all, He is all-knowing and all-powerful. But maybe, just maybe, the bad thing that you blame God for is the very thing He did or allowed to happen to you to save you from what He knows "would be." Just because we think something should be doesn't mean it would be. Should we possibly change the blame we have for God and simply say "thank you" and go on about our way?

Could it be that when things seem to be farthest from what we believe they should be, is when God is most involved preventing the devastation that would be?

Be intentional, be engaged, be interactive. Be a Red Fox Father.

FIFTEEN MINUTES OF FAME

Billy Rae Cyrus from *"Achy Breaky Heart"* comes to mind. John Marr Karr, who confessed to killing JonBenet Ramsey, that was his fifteen minutes. James Frey, author of *A Million Little Pieces*, had his although Oprah was not amused. My personal list goes on, remember Steve Bartman, the Cubs fan who interfered with a foul ball in the World Series dashing the Cubs hopes? Monica Lewinsky, or, to reach back even further, Joey Buttafuoco, and John Bobbit?

You might have been lucky enough to not have had your fifteen minutes yet, but for me, I remember what I call my fifteen minutes of fame. I think that I blew it, completely wasted it. I was about twelve years old, and my church group had driven up from Tallahassee, Florida, to Atlanta to watch a Braves game in Fulton County Stadium. It was a beautiful summer day, and the Braves were getting killed. I remember the stadium was packed that day, and I was bored, so I singlehandedly started the wave. It went around eight times and the Braves rallied and ended up winning the game. OK, the last part was pure embellishment, but it really jazzes the story up a bit. Nevertheless, that day I led 50,000 people to happiness, all eyes were on me, it was my fifteen minutes of fame. Unfortunately, I later realized that I wasted my fifteen minutes on a baseball game starting the wave. Had I known that I only had fifteen minutes, I assure you on that day I would have sat on my hands and opted for higher quality fifteen minutes.

I once worked with a man that who sat the bench for five NBA basketball games, remembered it like it was yesterday. He recalled how he was called up, warmed up with the "pros" (he was one at that point), and then watched five games from the bench . . . fifteen minutes. I also worked with a man who was drafted by the New England Patriots in 1984. He caught eleven passes in the NFL and spent a year or two injured, never returned. He described each catch in detail and hearing him discuss his experience was like being there yourself. You should have seen his face when I asked him about it . . . fifteen minutes.

Not long ago my kids were at the end of my last nerve and tickling it feverishly. It wasn't anything big that they were doing, it was more like a mosquito constantly buzzing around me. Not bad until you consider that mosquitoes are annoying little creatures, many of them bloodsuckers, who also carry diseases like malaria, Lyme disease, and hepatitis and all sorts of other problems. It was kind of like that. I know what you are thinking: "not from the Red Fox Father!" I hear ya, the whole be intentional, engaged, and interactive thing, but, hey, we are all human, and I didn't want to be engaged at this point. I needed some time.

Anyway, the kids were bothering me, and I needed a break, so I took a time out and totally rationalized it by comparing my dad techniques to all the people that I know whom work too much and don't spend quality time with their kids. It didn't work. You see, I have a little problem. I am writing a book that makes me always attempt to think of things in a different way. So I did. I figured that my kids will live with me for twenty-two years (maybe), and I will live to be eighty years old (maybe). This is 25% of my life . . . about fifteen minutes out of an hour. This is all you get, two innings of a baseball game, six outs. Heck, you are not even sure that you will get up to bat in two innings and if you are batting a respectable 300, chances are if you do get an at bat, you won't get on base. Fifteen minutes. That is all we have to build confidence, give life instruction, demonstrate wisdom. Don't blow it.

Fifteen minutes. I sure hope that we are not just starting the wave at a baseball game.

Anybody can be great for fifteen minutes, just ask Billy Rae. Go be a great dad, it only takes fifteen minutes.

Be intentional, be engaged, be interactive. Be a Red Fox Father.

BRICK IN THE WALL

August 13, 1961, marked the beginning of the Berlin Wall. This wall was erected to separate the communist government of East Germany from the democracy that was being created by the West Germans. The Wall was eighty-seven miles long and in 1962 the East Germans moved 110 yards east of the Wall and built a parallel fence establishing a "No Man's Land" in between the two. West Germans who worked in East Germany had to find new jobs in West Germany, families found themselves totally split, and visitation in the 60's was not allowed; the Wall separated everything.

Consider a wife and husband as two neighboring countries. I think that in my marriage I sometimes am building a wall in between my wife and me. Every time I hurt her, fail her expectations, disappoint her, or generally irritate her, she places a brick in the wall with a reasonable amount of concrete to ensure its security and tenure. Not only do I not object to the newly placed brick, I engage in a fair amount of my own masonry. Brick by brick the Marital Wall slowly gets built, both sides contributing.

When a couple meets, they find they have a lot in common, and they are living in Camelot, sharing, caring, and marrying. Then, because neither is perfect and the expectations are very high, and not stated, each time one hurts the other or something goes not according to the plan, a brick is laid along the border. The Wall begins. For each hurt or disappointment another brick goes in the wall. A couple of years means a couple more bricks, and neither party is interested in knocking his or her brick down. The bottom bricks have now set in: the concrete is dry, and the two parties that started out loving each other don't even notice the waist-high wall that they are creating. A couple more years go by of not living an intentional marriage, and the once euphoric couple is now having to raise chins just to see each other over The Wall. Soon they are yelling across the wall about even the most tiny of things, and before you know it, we have "No Man's Land." A communication barrier exists, neither party willing to make a move; diplomacy is futile. The caring and sharing are gone. It is too difficult, too many bricks. Some are lucky enough to find a third country to assist in the diplomatic process whereas some turn to all out war and call up an army of lawyers to demonstrate shock and awe to the neighboring country. The carpet bombing ensues.

Funny how we can treat a stranger with more kindness than our spouse. Not funny at all, but consider, no bricks and no walls . . . yet. The biggest problem is when something relatively tiny happens involving your neighboring country (spouse), and all you see is the other bricks (hurts and disappointments), and now you are angry. It wasn't the little thing. It was the little thing compounded by having to communicate it over the brick wall. After children enter the picture the bricks get bigger because the decisions become more important. Now, instead of deciding where we are going to eat, we have to decide how are we going to discipline, raise, and educate our children. Money matters and in-laws are also large bricks. The Wall construction gains momentum.

Before you go trying to knock down the bricks, just try to stop bricklaying. Don't feel like you have to make some sort of huge announcement at a press conference; just simply stop laying bricks. If you make an announcement, you have just set yet another standard you will fail to meet in the other country's eyes. Just stop laying bricks quietly. What is so important that you have to lay a brick anyway? Make some concessions. If the West Germans want you to lower the toilet seat, stop fighting, lower the toilet seat. It is one less brick in the wall. The wall takes a lot longer to build if only one of the countries is contributing the bricks. You can't control the other side's brick production the best thing to do is to not respond to her bricks with bricks of your own. You are the man; be bigger than the problem. Some of the best advice that I think that I have ever given was at my brother's wedding where I was the best man. I don't recall everything that I said, although I am sure it was wonderful. However, I do remember saying something like "the key to a good marriage is not just knowing all the right things to say, but, more importantly, knowing when to say nothing at all." No comment, no brick; save it for more important negotiations. If you find yourself with a chin-high brick wall, try treating your neighboring country a little more like a stranger. We all are generally nice to strangers, and it might loosen the mortar a bit.

Brick busting is very difficult, but remember the Berlin Wall was knocked down in November of 1989, almost thirty years later. It wasn't easy to get there, and it didn't happen overnight. Nearly 200 people were shot trying to cross the Wall. Don't attempt to knock down the entire wall with a dozen roses or one night in Vegas. To brick bust, apologize. Although she laid some of the bricks, you know you have some responsibility in creating them too. Heck you might have mixed the concrete yourself. Apologize specifically. Although the generic "I am a man and I am sorry" seems to bust a couple of bricks, try naming the areas that you totally screwed up on. You might even throw in a couple of things that you were right on but reacted poorly about during the negotiations. You know what you have done, and, yes, you are guilty, too. I know this because chances are high she told you when you screwed up. Be a man, apologize, and be bigger than the problem.

I also think that it is important to not feel as if I need to convince my spouse that my points are right or what I am saying is accurate all the time. I need to allow her to be able to disagree. Eventually, the truth or correct direction shows itself with enough time. Consider that God did not put your wife in your life so you can fix her. Maybe God put your wife in your life so HE can fix you.

Fathers, be intentional in your relationship with your spouse, slow to anger, prudent with your wife's trust because if you don't it could be another brick in the wall.

Be intentional, be engaged, be interactive. Be a Red Fox Father.

DOMINOES

Seems as if dominoes are just not as popular as they were when I was a kid. I am not referring to people actually playing the game. If you are about my age, you probably remember television shows during which some guy spent hours, sometimes days standing up dominoes just to push that first domino over and watch that one single domino send off a chain reaction that knocked down thousands of dominoes. Some would climb stairs and flip into the air, and some would drop in water and after a delayed reaction send more dominoes tumbling down the line. I was always awed when that one special domino would fall and send dominoes tumbling in more than one direction simultaneously. The guy who built the whole domino maze was ever so careful not to touch the dominoes in case he knocked one over. But the real trick was that first one. That was the most important domino because it started the whole event, and the event was spectacular. I don't know what it was, but something just seemed to draw me to those shows and I would sit in utter amazement of how it all worked together, beginning with just one simple domino. The irony here is that the whole concept of actually playing the game of dominoes is blocking. Dominoes is a game in which the victory goes to the player who can block the other player from moving his dominoes.

Sometimes it's funny how life works, sometimes it isn't. I have a friend whom I highly respect. He is a father of three with a wonderful wife, a professional career-minded individual who has done well with money and has what seems to be the perfect life. At least he did until that first domino fell and the sequence of events that followed destroyed everything he worked so hard to obtain. My friend had an affair.

Actually, the affair was not the first domino, Red Fox Fathers. The affair was the domino towards the end of the event that sent dominoes tumbling in multiple directions. The first domino was just a single innocent little domino that my friend pushed too far, which subsequently pushed another domino, and thinking this was fun, another, and then another. After a couple hundred dominoes, my friend was in a situation that he couldn't even stop. Dominoes were falling everywhere.

As we men get a little older and our hair begins to grey or even fall out, our muscle definition fades, and our bellies become less like a six pack and more like a two liter, our confidence seems to wander off, and we start to pay attention to the Cialis commercials. When somebody shows a little interest in this middle-aged man, the whole situation can be enticing and fun and can make him feel a little better about himself. I will never be convinced that my friend woke up one morning and thought, "Today I am going to have sex with a co-worker." However, it did all start with that first domino. A conversation turned flirtatious that he thought was harmless and a little fun. Then a lunch under the cloak of "it's business" that turned personal. Before he knew it, they were Facebook friends, email buds, and let's not forget the texting. You say anything when you're texting and leave it up to the other party to interpret. She shared her problems, and he was an empathetic ear or he shared his problems, and she was an empathetic ear. Before he or she knew it, they were a couple hundred dominoes down the road, and watching those dominoes fall was spectacular. They were drawn to it. The one string of dominoes falling at a time became not as exciting and not quite as much fun anymore, so they needed more, and before you knew it they were not just talking anymore. As dominoes tumble more tumble and there is my friend fully involved with another woman and she with him all because they pushed one domino too far and the string of events were just too much to stop. He never considered the future because he never saw any future. The irony to this whole situation was that he saw somebody who wanted him physically, and the only real reason why she wanted him physically is because of the life she thought he might possibly provide, the very life his wife was living. Two people hopeful for a life that wouldn't exist. She didn't really want him physically, but it was a means to an end. He had no intention of leaving his wife; the affair was just an ego boost. But you don't have time to discuss these things when the dominoes are moving. You just have to sit back and watch the excitement of the controlled chaos controlled until one domino gets away and the whole thing comes crashing down, his wife found out and left. Dominoes are now everywhere. His relationship with his children was completely destroyed. He created three children of a broken home; a lifelong identity unearned, unwelcome, and undesirable. Red Fox Fathers, stop here and think about this for a minute. I have firsthand knowledge of this identity; it's a life changer no matter what they try to tell you. His wife probably will never trust again, forever scarred and bitter by the event. A man who was once a Red Fox Father now only has the hopes of being spoken to on holidays or maybe receiving a phone call if he forgets to mail in the child support check.

The key to avoid all of it is simple: avoid <u>all</u> of it. You don't have to get up every morning and worry about all those dominoes, just the first one. Red Fox Fathers, remember the affair was not the first domino; it was towards the end. In order for all the other dominoes to fall, the first one has to fall, so if you keep the first domino from falling, all the other dominoes will still peacefully stand. Practical advice to keep the first domino from falling is simple. Don't get involved personally with people of the opposite sex. Should a woman engage in a flirtatious comment, don't reply; it's not necessary. If a woman brings to you a personal problem and needs a kind ear, recommend that she talk to a person of the same sex. Avoid lunch with females, and if you do have to have a business lunch with a female, bring somebody else. Two's company, and three's a crowd. Don't put yourself in a situation where you have your finger on the first domino shaking back and forth. Close your Facebook page. If you feel you have to have a Facebook page, then offer to share one with your wife or give her your password. Allow your wife to scroll through your text messages, phone book, or email anytime she wants. Don't see this as her not trusting you; see it as her needing security in the relationship and accountability. If you are thinking you need to delete a text as you hit the send button, then don't send the text. That's the first domino. Trying to be funny or flirtatious or giving somebody the wrong signal is like wiggling that first domino. Don't do it. If you think that your wife no longer finds you physically attractive, then consider these harsh words: maybe you're not. If you're not to her, then you are most likely not to the other woman; she just wants the life your wife has, not necessarily you. You are a means to an end.

Two of the most pernicious ways to knock that first domino over are simple and simple to avoid. First, avoid convincing yourself that an affair would be your wife's fault for not meeting your needs. Don't let those thoughts in your head. The blame game is for weak men, and if you truly believe that your wife is not meeting your needs and you should have an affair, start trying to meet her needs. Control your decision, and don't then tell your wife that she controlled your decision. The second way to knock that domino over is to convince yourself you are immune from falling into the cycle. Until scientists come up with some potion that cures the male libido, you can't knock over a few dominoes and then stop the whole process. Once dominoes fall, it's what dominoes do. Avoid engaging in just a couple of dominoes falling. You can't stop it once it starts and don't try to convince yourself that you are different. You're not.

Red Fox Fathers, you have a duty to keep the fidelity in your marriage and to keep your children living in your same house. Be aggressively intentional about avoiding that first domino. Remember, to win at dominoes, it is all about blocking.

Be intentional, be engaged, be interactive. Be a faithful Red Fox Father.

MISSION DIFFICULT

O ne of my favorite lines in *Mission Impossible* is when Ethan Hunt was given his next mission. Ethan says it was going to be very difficult. The mission commander replies, "Mr. Hunt, this isn't mission difficult, it's mission impossible. 'Difficult' should be a walk in the park for you."

I feel that good fatherhood should be on *Mission Impossible*. Consider the challenges. Retaining employment, matching the hours that your peers work, making time to have a working relationship with your wife, competing with the TV and XBox for your children's time and admiration, not getting a regular dose of sex even though it is readily available outside of marriage, and raising children in a society that is completely geared to guide them to destruction. Yes, I think it is that bad. Can't you just hear the theme music? Difficult, very, but this isn't Mission Difficult, it is *Mission Impossible*, and if Ethan Hunt can do it, so can we.

As a father of two daughters, I believe that a large part of my mission is to get my daughters safely to their wedding day. At that point, some young man takes over meeting her every need, or at least he better. That is my plan; I doubt that it is his. Another thing that I believe is that my daughter will eventually compare every boyfriend to me. My mission, should I choose to accept it, is to make it as difficult as possible for some young man that doesn't have respect for women to get involved in her life. Difficult? No, make it impossible! One day she will be a tough-to-deal with, and unreasonable teenager, so the only way to accomplish this is to set a subconscious high standard in her world now. How do you do this? **Be the type of husband you want your daughter to marry**.

Between my neighbor and I we have four daughters. We have on occasion discussed that when it comes time for our daughters to date, we would conveniently be together cleaning our guns, discussing our time in jail, or being generally mean and intimidating. I remember one father telling me how he made his daughter's suitors leave twenty dollars behind. It was returned when the young man returned the daughter before curfew; if not, it cost him twenty bucks. I thought that was a creative idea, but I am not sure I am comfortable with trading twenty dollars for my daughter; considering inflation and all. So the Red Fox Father did some research and found on the internet some easy to follow rules for potential suitors that all young men should follow.

1. If you pull into my driveway and honk you'd better be delivering a package, because you're sure not picking anything up.
2. You do not touch my daughter in front of me. You may glance at her, so long as you do not peer at anything below her neck. If you cannot keep your eyes or hands off of my daughter's body, I will remove them from yours.
3. I am aware that it is considered fashionable for boys of your age to wear trousers so loosely that they appear to be falling off your hips. Please don't take this as an insult, but

THE RED FOX FATHER

you and all of your friends are complete idiots. Still, I want
to be fair and open minded about this issue, so I propose
this compromise: You may come to the door with your
underwear showing and your pants ten sizes too big, and
I will not object. However, in order to ensure that your
clothes do not, in fact, come off during the course of your
date with my daughter, I will take my electric nail gun
and fasten your trousers securely in place to your waist.

4. I'm sure you've been told that in today's world, sex without
   utilizing a "barrier method" of some kind can kill you.
   Let me elaborate, when it comes to sex, I am the barrier,
   and I will kill you.

5. It is usually understood that in order for us to get to
   know each other, we should talk about sports, politics,
   and other issues of the day. Please do not do this. The
   only information I require from you is an indication of
   when you expect to have my daughter safely back at my
   house, and the only word I need from you on this subject
   is "early."

6. I have no doubt you are a popular fellow with many
   opportunities to date other girls. This is fine with me as
   long as it is okay with my daughter. Otherwise, once you
   have gone out with my little girl, you will continue to date
   no one but her until she is finished with you. If you make
   her cry, I will make you cry.

7. As you stand in my front hallway, waiting for my daughter
   to appear, and more than an hour goes by, do not sigh and
   fidget. If you want to be on time for the movie, you should
   not be dating. My daughter is putting on her makeup, a
   process than can take longer than painting the Golden
   Gate Bridge. Instead of just standing there, why don't you
   do something useful, like changing the oil in my car?

8. The following places are not appropriate for a date with my daughter: places where there are beds, sofas, or anything softer than a wooden stool; places where there is darkness; places where there is dancing, holding hands, or happiness; places where the ambient temperature is warm enough to induce my daughter to wear shorts, tank tops, midriff T-shirts, or anything other than overalls, a sweater, and a goose down parka—zipped up to her throat. Movies with a strong romantic or sexual theme are to be avoided; movies that features sports are okay. Hockey games are okay. Old folks homes are better.

9. Do not lie to me. I may appear to be a potbellied, balding, middle-aged, dimwitted has-been. But on issues relating to my daughter, I am the all-knowing, merciless god of your universe. If I ask you where you are going and with whom, you have one chance to tell me the truth, the whole truth and nothing but the truth. I have a shotgun, a shovel, and five acres behind the house. Do not trifle with me.

10. Be afraid. Be very afraid. It takes very little for me to mistake the sound of your car in the driveway for an terrorist attack. As soon as you pull into the driveway you should exit the car with both hands in plain sight. Speak the perimeter password, announce in a clear voice that you have brought my daughter home safely and early, then return to your car—there is no need for you to come inside. The camouflaged face at the window is mine.

Unfortunately, I don't think that my wife will allow the rules to be discussed with the potential person who is going to try to ruin my life. I would guess my daughter wouldn't like it either, but she doesn't get an opinion on this matter. This leaves me with only one option left: to be on the date with them. Now, get this, I am not as crazy as you all might think. I don't really mean physically be on the date; I mean subconsciously. What type of guy do you want your daughter to eventually marry? Answer that question, and that is the type of husband you need to be. It's that simple. Set the bar high, Dad, and you will find you will be a much more pleased grandfather.

Good morning. Your mission, should you choose to accept it, involves making any potential suitor of your daughter's hand meet a very high standard of respect and love. You may select any two team members, but it is essential that the third member of your team be your wife. She is a civilian and a highly capable professional mother. You have eighteen years to accomplish this mission. As always, should any member of your team be caught or killed, the secretary will disavow all knowledge of your actions. This message will self-destruct in five seconds.

Be intentional, be engaged, be interactive. Be a Red Fox Father. Make it your mission.

THE MONEY YOU COULD BE SAVING WITH GEICO

When I first heard GEICO's new advertising campaign, the businessman came out in me. I couldn't help but think what a waste of money the new campaign was. The gecko had such momentum, nationally known, all over billboards. I bet they had little gecko stuffed animals, key chains, coffee mugs, the works. Now, they have to change thousands of billboards, trinkets, production for radio, TV, print, etc. Yet when they came out with a stack of money with eyeballs on it, it seemed to work. I guess I conceded my original misperception when an employee of mine came to work singing "Somebody's Watching Me" and then said, "That's just the money you could be saving with GEICO". When I heard this, I figured the new ad campaign was going to stick.

However, when I see the commercial with the music from Rockwell, "*Somebody's Watching Me,*" I can't help but think about when my kids were younger. Just in case you don't remember from when your kids were younger, every time you are in the bathroom at home with small children, it seems like the children seek you out like a smart bomb heading towards a terrorist's bedroom window. They seek you out with laser like accuracy from 150 miles away; they are <u>always</u> watching you.

Often when I am calling my son for a chore or to discipline him, I wonder if his sense of hearing is totally shot. It seems as if he is completely deaf; he definitely has a unique ability to ignore me. But, nonetheless, I on several occasions have decided to check his hearing by saying something like "cake" or "cookie" just to make sure that his hearing is ok. It is. My son had multiple ear infections as a child, so my concern for his hearing is genuine. My daughter, though, has the same situation going on. I can instruct her to her face while she is looking at me in the eyes and ask her to repeat what I just said five seconds earlier and she has no idea.

Bottom line, I am worried about my children not listening to me.

One thing that I really found disturbing was when my daughter started verbally snapping at people. It wasn't all the time, but if her mother or I went to remind her of something she already knew, she would snap back, "I KNOW THAT!" My wife and I were confused; why did she do this? Where did she learn this from? Of course, in my world, my children learn all of their bad habits from other children at school, never from home. So my wife and I coached her, "Honey, when somebody reminds you of something you already know, you don't have to answer so aggressively, just simply say, "Thank you for reminding me." Well the chicken came home to roost the other day when I was heading out for a business trip and spent a decent amount of time packing. My wife, in an attempt to help, decided to remind me yet again to take something with me. The first thing in my head, you guessed it, "I KNOW THAT!" To my credit, I stopped the words just as my teeth were parting. A light of wisdom glowed down on my head like when Moses parted the Red Sea. In that moment of time, I finally opted to use wisdom, so I responded, "Thank you for reminding me." I was pleased with myself for not putting a "brick in the wall" but it was then I realized that my daughter picked up her little snappy attitude from me, not the heathens at her school. All this time she was just emulating me. It was then I decided that I needed to worry less about my child's inability to listen and concern myself more with her super ability to observe.

Red Fox Fathers, I assure you somebody is indeed watching you, and it's not just the money you could be saving with GEICO. They may not be good listeners but they make great watchers and consider your actions are speaking louder than words.

Be intentional, be engaged, be interactive. Be a Red Fox Father.

Follow the Yellow Brick Road

I generally try to direct my children's lives. I can tell the older they get, the more control I lose and the more they push against the boundaries that I set for them. My wife says that discipline should be like an upside-down funnel: be very strict at first like the narrow end of the funnel and in the later years you can widen the funnel and be less strict. Her philosophy is that this method is easier than not being strict at first and having to become strict later. You can always loosen the grip, but it is really difficult to tighten the nozzle.

I do question regularly if I am directing them in the right way, teaching them how to think for themselves, be confident, and socialize effectively. Nonetheless, no matter if I am right or wrong, at this stage of their lives, I am pulling all the levers and pushing all the buttons. When I think about the responsibility they have given me, at times I get somewhat overwhelmed with my task. I would guess that I am similar to most fathers, but, unfortunately, I most likely am not. As I talk to other dads, I am amazed that they have children at all. The consensus seems that our job is just to get our sons to eighteen, or get our daughters married, simply put the "Follow the Yellow Brick Road" mentality. Just keep traveling down the road, and your children will eventually get to

Oz. Moving through time until the children are adults and we can retire. I think that my job as father is much greater than that. I have eighteen to twenty-two years to prepare them for the next fifty plus years of living.

I still remember the first time that I saw *The Wizard of Oz*. I was scared. Every time the Wicked Witch showed up, I ran behind the couch to hide. Now, to save face, I will tell you I was a little boy, but this event was so dramatic for me that I still remember it today. My father was sitting on the couch, and I didn't make it through the entire movie; I went to my room.

For those of you that don't remember the movie; Dorothy gets swept up in a tornado and finds herself in a different place, the Land of Oz. She accidentally killed the Wicked Witch's sister and just wanted to get back to Kansas. To do this she had to follow the Yellow Brick Road, sounds simple enough, but along her travels she met the Tin Man, that needed a heart, the Lion, that needed courage, and the Scarecrow that needed a brain. Together all of them needed to get to the great Wizard to get what they needed and all this time the Wicked Witch and a bunch of Flying Monkeys were out to get them.

After following the Yellow Brick Road, being chased by the Wicked Witch, the Flying Monkeys and getting distracted numerous times they finally arrive in Oz and meet the Wizard. Now the Wizard is no real Wizard, he is just an old man that has put on quite a show with smoke and fire by pulling levers and pushing buttons to make the "Wizard" look really great in an effort to advise our young travelers and convince them of his great wisdom. When our travelers found out the Wizard was no Wizard, but just an old man behind a curtain pulling levers and pushing buttons, they find themselves extremely disappointed. They lost all confidence in his ability to advise them, he no longer had wisdom in their eyes. The old man then had to convince our young travelers that he did have the answers and the wisdom to still direct them to help them attain their goals; a heart, courage, a brain, and of course, back to Kansas.

I think that parents want their children to get to the Land of Oz. During their travels, evil people, like the wicked witch will try to keep them from it. These children will make some friends along the way, and some of these friends will lack brains, heart, and courage. Your children will get detoured, but eventually they will get there. While they are young, as a father, you will be pulling the levers and pushing their buttons and they will think that you are some great wizard. As they become teenagers, they will discover that you are just an old man behind that curtain, but perhaps by then you will be able to convince them that you are still the great Wizard, just without the smoke and fire.

The bottom line is this, Red Fox Father: your children are not in Kansas anymore. As they follow the yellow brick road of life, there will be plenty of wicked witches, flying monkeys, and a couple of crazy friends. Now is the time to make sure that you are pulling the **right** levers and pressing the **right** buttons, for soon enough they will no longer think that you are some great wizard, but just an old man behind a curtain. If you can instill in them the wisdom of the great wizard early, maybe they will be able to listen to the old man later. Before you click your heels three times, they will become teenagers, and lets hope they will still be able to pay attention to the old man behind the curtain. If not at first, don't give up. After all, at one point, you were the Great Wizard, and life is not as easy as just following the yellow brick road.

Be intentional, be engaged, be interactive. Be a Red Fox Father.

THE CHOICE

In the movie *The Matrix*, our hero, Neo, finds himself in an old wooden chair and is asked to choose between the blue pill and the red pill. Choose the blue pill and everything returns to normal, choose the red pill and the truth will be revealed to you. I would guess that most of us would chose the red pill. After all for most of us, reality as we know it is not that great and man is constantly seeking the truth. Why am I here? What is going to happen? What is my purpose? The blue pill is boring, the same old same old; the red pill is exciting, something new, the unknown. The key to the choice proposed to Neo is that, there is no going back: once the choice is made, the choice is made.

How many times in our lives have we sat in that same chair making a choice? Job change, dating choices, illegal drug use, education, what house to buy, business ventures, being unfaithful in our marriage . . . all are decisions that require a heavy dose of wisdom and a side order of patience because once you swallow that pill, there is no going back. Just the fact that the other day I decided to linger at a stoplight and not turn right immediately led to my vehicle's trunk lid inside of another vehicle's hood. Choices. I realize that I have had to make tougher decisions than my father and grandfather, and our kids will most likely make tougher decisions than we have had to make. Red Fox Fathers, the time to equip our children for their turn in that chair starts today.

I am in a position at work that manages a couple hundred people. Now this brings a tremendous number of challenges to my life because people are challenging. One thing that seems to happen more often than I prefer is that if an employee has a personal situation that affects their work, and most serious situations do, they feel the need to air out these problems sitting on the other side of my desk. I have had to learn to be a decent listener over the years, but through all of this, I have come to the conclusion that a great many of the problems that people have are from bad choices that have been made. They have done it to themselves, and the wiser ones can see the errors of their ways. After all, hindsight is truly twenty twenty. There have been many who blame their problems on the world, God, parents, kids, you name it. Most of the time these excuses are nothing more than bystanders who find themselves within blaming distance.

I figure that I have learned something great here and have decided that it is important for my children to understand a couple of things. First, they must make wise choices, and second, choices have consequences. Seems like basic knowledge, however, many people don't understand this concept. So what was I doing to make sure my children learned this the easy way in lieu of life training? I was doing nothing.

Recently my son has been having discipline issues and has received an increased amount of punishment. He put great thought into his situation and decided it was time to tell me that he no longer wanted me to give him punishment. I acquiesced to his request. I would no longer decide when he received punishment; he would.

This is how it worked: the next time he engaged in behavior that was unacceptable, I told him, "If you choose to continue to (*bad behavior here*) you will receive punishment. If you choose to no longer (*bad behavior here*) there will be no punishment. The choice and outcome are yours. Choose wisely." Oddly enough, at four years of age, he was able to use deductive reasoning and make the right choice.

In addition to choosing whether or not he receives punishment, I have expanded his decision-making authority to other things. I merely point out on occasion that he is making a decision. For example, when we eat out, his meal decision is one that eliminates other options. *Choose wisely.* Play time is the same way; playing with trains eliminates baseball. *Choose wisely.* With every situation I can, I am empowering him to make his own decision. Although the decisions are somewhat insignificant now, I am also teaching him that these very same decisions come with consequences. *Choose wisely.* He is fast becoming more thoughtful with his decisions and not randomly moving through his day; I can see the wheels spinning and the light bulb beginning to flicker. My hope is that when he is fifteen and some kid wants him to try illegal drugs, he considers the consequences and chooses wisely.

I can't tell you for sure what was going through Neo's head, if anything. I am not certain that Neo has been taught that choices matter, that many have no return, and that all have consequences, Neo might be succumbing to peer pressure or acting "in the moment"; maybe he just knows all the other kids are doing it. For my son, I don't want any of these three options to be foundations upon which he makes decisions.

Red Fox Fathers, every day you too have a choice. Every day you choose to either be engaged in your child's life or to be a bystander who will find himself one day within blaming distance for all of life's problems that come your child's way. If you make no choice, you have chosen. The choice is made for you, and, remember, choices matter. This one has no return, and inaction will have consequences. Choose wisely.

Don't let your child be that employee sitting across from his boss blaming you because he or she made some bad choices and now life is falling apart. Life is tough enough, choose wisely.

Choose to be intentional, choose to be engaged, choose to be interactive. Choose to be a Red Fox Father.

UNDER PRESSURE

I am sure we all remember hearing our parents say at one time or another, "If I have said it once, I have said it a thousand times." If I had a nickel for every time my mother said that . . . well, let's just say I would have a lot of nickels. She said it a lot, and looking back, I can tell you that she should have because she was consistently repeating the same directions, consistently communicating the same wisdom, and consistent dispensing the same discipline. I remember as I grew a little bit older I eventually just told her, "Just quit saying it then." She never did; consistent pressure.

Currently my wife and I are in the process of trying to help our daughter break the habit of sucking her thumb. This is no easy task, mind you; the child has been sucking her thumb since she was in the womb and I have the ultrasound picture to prove it. My daughter is very inquisitive and has to know why, and I feel it necessary to tell my children why I ask them to do certain things. So when she asked why I didn't want her to suck her thumb, I found a great opportunity to dispense some of my fatherhood wisdom. I replied, "Honey, if you keep sucking your thumb, your teeth will grow straight out of you mouth and come in all crooked." Again, she replied, "why?" so I went further: "Because, darling, your thumb applies incremental consistent pressure to your teeth and although it is only a small amount of pressure, once applied in a consistent direction against your teeth, the pressure from your thumb will push your teeth out." I happen to believe that the same holds true in raising children: incremental consistent pressure, applied in a consistent direction, will yield results. Yes, you better believe that is what I told my daughter, whether she understood it or not, she will understand it eventually, but only if I am consistent.

I will be the first to admit that I get very tired of providing the same direction over and over and over again. Not just the important stuff, the simple things as well. Seems as if every night I have to tell her to brush her teeth about twenty times; I wonder when is she just going to get it? It is as if every five seconds stand on their own. She reminds me of the character Dory in the movie *Finding Nemo*. Dory was the bluefish that Nemo's father, Marlin, met and partnered with to find Nemo. The problem was that Dory suffered from short term memory loss, I mean real short term, like five seconds or less. So it goes like this: I tell my daughter to brush her teeth and within five seconds, something else has her attention and the event repeats. Even though I get tired of constantly repeating myself doesn't mean I let her get to a point where I no longer tell her to brush her teeth.

The important thing to remember here is that it is not about brushing her teeth, it is about all the other things that I need to tell her that I don't consistently tell her. Incremental consistent pressure, applied in a consistent direction, will yield the desired results. I guess that I am releasing myself from having to "fix" my daughter or teach her everything that she needs to know on the first try. This leaves me a lot less frustrated, which keeps me from giving up and also helps me to remember I can concede the little situations, just so long as I remember to continue the consistent pressure. Again, incremental consistent pressure, applied in a consistent direction, will yield the desired results. I live to instruct another day, and the results that I am looking for, although not instantly attained, are one conversation closer to reality. The one thing to remember is that if you are consistent with your direction, instruction, discipline, eventually your child will have an "aha" moment, and the results will be attained. Even teeth are no match for incremental, consistent pressure.

For those of you with teenagers, although it is frustrating, try not to get frustrated. Don't take your eye off the goal and that is incremental consistent pressure in a consistent direction. Come on too strong and they will see you coming, and the counter pressure intensifies in the opposite direction. Pressure, when applied incrementally, has the power to move things, teenagers and teeth included. Just keep on keeping on and you will get your results.

If you didn't see *Finding Nemo*, I will tell you that eventually Dory has to remember something. She is charged with remembering the address of where little Nemo can be found. How she accomplishes this is to repeat the address over and over and over again. Get the point? Consistency!

Red Fox Fathers, being consistent for eighteen to twenty years is difficult. If you want little Nemo to be OK, and every father does, using consistent direction, consistent discipline, and providing consistent wisdom will get you there. Apply them with incremental pressure and one day you will arrive where Dory and Marlin do, at

P Sherman
42 Wallaby Way
Sydney, Austrailia

and Nemo will be saved.

Be consistently intentional, be consistently engaged, be consistently interactive. Be consistently a Red Fox Father.

WHAT CAN BROWN DO FOR YOU?

R ecently, a friend, in a weak moment, told me that he had not only watched QVC, but had actually purchased from QVC. For those real men out there who do not know what QVC is, it is a shopping network on television. I, representing men everywhere, immediately revoked three "Man Cards" from my friend. His penitence was to watch three SportCenters and attend one NFL football game.

I will admit that I have purchased some items from a website before. I would guess that most of us have, it just wasn't QVC. I still consider Amazon moderately manly. Once the order is placed I receive a plethora of emails tracking my package throughout its various stops as it travels the countryside. I feel the anticipation build as the package gets closer and more emails come my way. It is almost as if the package is keeping a journal of its travels and writing home to tell the story.

Dear New Owner,

Today I was at a distribution facility in Topeka, Kansas. I saw vast country estates, farms, and wheat fields. I have met a lot of people that are being very nice to me. I look forward to coming home, though, and will be on your doorstep this Thursday before 10:30 am.

Sincerely,
New Package

I then look very forward to the UPS guy's arrival. Not that he is special; nor even a friend of mine, I just think the guy is a little like Santa Claus in a way. I know that I paid for the package, but that was 3-5 days ago, and now I just have a strange man, who knows where I live, and knows what I want coming to my house. Even better he is dropping that very item on my doorstep. I have to say, I look up to that guy. I even at times wonder if he knows if I've been naughty or nice.

So this guy comes to my door, drops the package, turns his back, walks completely away, and forgets the package ever existed because he knows, he now has more important packages inside his truck. Plain and simple, I can respect that. You see, I would like to drop packages at my front door, too. Follow me here; I come home from work with packages. Not wrapped nicely in a box, my packages are burdens: the economy is weak, my employer is not doing that well, my boss is stressed and takes it out on me, my coworker disrespects me, I have too much work, too little time, my employees are insubordinate, I don't make enough money to pay the bills and you name it. I have packages. The one thing that I need to do is learn a lesson from my UPS guy and leave them at the doorstep and walk away. The only difference is that I leave them at the doorstep before I walk in, not head back to a truck. Some days are really bad, and I have to pause for a moment to drop off all the packages at the door before entry. I know that once I enter the home my little boy and my little girls deserve a daddy who is not still carrying packages of this nature. They need their daddy 100% focused, 100% available, 100% package free. My son has no idea that the economy is bad. My daughter is not aware that the business I work for is about to go under. It is not their fault that they are happy and ready for daddy time. Pause for a moment, fathers; drop the packages at the doorstep, and then walk in because you need to be ready for your children. Whereas our wives understand somewhat what we all face every day, our children don't, so when you come home still carrying a burden, they have no sense to give you space, grace, and not get in your face. What can Brown do for me? Leave the package at the door and walk away because the truth is that you have more important packages inside.

Be intentional, be engaged, be interactive. Be a Red Fox Father, package free.

There Is An App For That

I remember when my uncle got a cell phone for work. It was huge by today's standards, and the battery was carried around in a bag. It wasn't really a cell phone, it was a car phone. That is what they were called back then, and they were rare. He received one because he was a traveling salesman and needed it for work. It was expensive per minute, and he had to use it sparingly.

The next time there was a cell phone in my life was when I finally got one. It was big as well, but the battery didn't need a bag. I remember it felt weird actually driving down the road and talking to my friends. For some strange reason, whenever somebody found out I was on a cell phone, they had to ask, "Where are you?" as if I weren't truly on a cell phone until I could tell the other party exactly where I was, and it couldn't be at home. I was in my twenties when I got my cell phone, so when I was in high school and making plans with people, we had to do exactly that, make plans. "Okay, I will meet you in the mall food court, next to Sbarros by the trash can at seven. If we don't meet up there, then the second place is outside the movie theater at 7:45 on the left wall." Or how about when you found out what happened at work over the weekend on Monday, instead of getting the phone calls/texts/emails all weekend long dealing with issues. The reason why you could wait until Monday is because generally nothing happened over the weekend. This was because nobody else had a cell phone either, so, nothing really happened until everybody came to work on Monday. Remember those days?

Now I feel naked without my cell phone. I have even driven home from work because I have forgotten my cell phone. Yes, I have an office phone, but you know how it is. I'd be willing to bet that you have done the same thing from time to time. Nowadays it seems that I am like a brain surgeon, always on call. Dinner with the family, I am on call, movie with my son, I am on call, intimate time with my wife, yep, I am on call. The real problem is that I have done it to myself. I have set others' expectations that if they call, I will answer.

This weekend I realized that on my priority list my cell phone is higher up than my son. I realized this because my son told me. What did he say? Nothing. It was his face when we were playing. I took a call and could see his disappointment. It wasn't even important; the phone rang, and like a good boy, I came running. It dawned on me, Red Fox Fathers, that we are first-generation cell phone fathers. My children have to compete with something I never had to deal with; and I don't know what it is like for my dad to put his cell phone above me. Sure, we had a home phone, but when we were anywhere but home, I had 100% attention. No cell phone, no email, no text, no games, no "apps for that"; there were no interruptions.

As a first-generation cell-phone father, I have never seen any advice on cell-phone use within the family. Don't misunderstand me; my wife has some regular advice. Apparently she is not a fan of

THE RED FOX FATHER

reading or typing on my smart phone when I am driving. Seems like a strange request since I have perfected this rare talent with hours of real-life practice. Other than that, no advice for first-generation cell phone fathers.

Given that I am trying to become a Red Fox Father, I have set the following guidelines. My cell phone works for me, I do not work for it. Just because it calls me does not mean that I have to come running like a slave to the airwaves. I am the owner; therefore, when I am engaged, interactive, and intentional with my children, I refuse to answer my cell phone. Should I feel as if it is an emergency, the boss or the wife or waiting on a call, I will politely excuse myself first from my interaction in lieu of just walking off, cell phone in hand. I am sure my children are observing my actions and my previous unwritten guidelines are being etched in my children's minds.

Right now my children are not old enough to have cell phones but there will come a day when I will be the one disappointed when they answer their cell phone. Imagine trying to assist my son with homework, or passing some great wisdom on to my daughters, and he or she reaches for the hip and, as fast a Captain Kirk, the cell phone flips open, "hello", all I will hear is "Dad, you're not important." First-generation cell-phone fathers, this is our future. Some of you are already experiencing it.

I will hold myself to these guidelines so my children, when teenagers, will understand not to be a slave to the cell phone. Yes, this means not reading the email or text or answering the cell-phone every time it beckons. Painful, yes, but necessary. This may be difficult for some of us who are absolutely addicted to the cell-phone and to being completely accessible. So if you need help, there is an app for that: it is called the power button. Shut it off. It's a great app when used properly.

Be intentional, be engaged, be interactive. Be a Red Fox Father.

STUPID IS AS STUPID DOES

I don't have much need for alcohol. Most of the people who get to know me realize that generally I stay in an altered state of mind regardless of the beverage I am drinking. I can't help it much, it just seems that since I have had children, I seem to be a little, shall I say, weird.

I have heard some of my friends say that teenagers will drive you to drink, at which point I wonder, when did you lose control? Oh, it is never one particular event, it is a process, a process that no father can ever prevent. Your only hope is to contain it.

My theory is this: when you have an infant, you just about encompass the child's entire world. Imagine that the child's world is the square. Let's call it the Square of Life, and your influence is the circle, or the Circle of Influence.

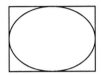

Notice the square is small, as is the child's world, and the circle occupies almost the entire square, which means you are in control. The only thing that you do not control is when the child poops, pees, and cries. Everything else is in your Circle of Influence: when he eats, where he lies, what toys are in his life, who can hold him, what he wears, whom he plays with, how long his hair is, etc. Even at this point the items outside your circle frustrate you. For example, if the baby cried all night last night, or if he urinated when you were changing his diaper. Frustrating, but it is still okay, you are in control of most everything else.

Now as your child becomes older, the Square of Life becomes bigger, as does your Circle of Influence, but not quite at the same rate.

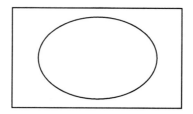

Now the child doesn't want to eat vegetables, doesn't want to go to bed, doesn't want to keep his room clean. He is meeting friends at school whom you don't know, playing by himself, beginning to read, and it goes on and on and on. Your Circle of Influence is waning, but still it is okay because you still control most of the more important items and you can control the consequences for the behavior you find unacceptable, thereby obtaining the desired responses. Plus, the child still needs you, and you are able to maintain the circle for the child's own safety. The key here is that at this point your child is smart: he realizes that he does not know everything and that "Father knows best." He may not say it but he still fears and respects you. Then something happens over time. He becomes a teenager, and teenagers are stupid. You most likely know this from experience. That is how I first learned this fact. I don't mean stupid in a mean way, I mean it in its truest definition. Teenagers are so ignorant; they think they know it all. Back to circles and squares. Imagine this square is all the wisdom in the world. Let's call this the Square of Knowledge, and the circle is the wisdom that a child possesses, or the Circle of Wisdom.

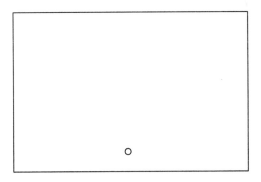

The circle encompasses the wisdom of the child. You are vastly wiser than the child, and at first the child knows this. Now as he becomes a teenager his Circle of Wisdom expands . . . a little.

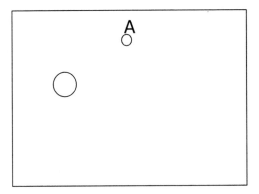

Even though his Circle of Wisdom is still very small relative to the Square of Knowledge, in his eyes he has become so much more aware, ten times wiser in a short period of time simply because his circle has become so much bigger relative to what it was. It is also important to note that wherever the walls of the Circle of Wisdom touches is what he knows, he doesn't know. I will explain, inside the circle is what he knows, what is outside the circle is what he doesn't know, and the perimeter of the circle, the part that touches the area inside the square, are the only parts of life that he knows he doesn't know. He does not realize that he actually knows very little; instead he believes he knows everything because in reality his circle is still very small. This is the reason why I say they are stupid: they don't even know what they don't know.

For example, where the small circle is, they are completely unaware (ignorant/stupid) that they don't know this particular piece of wisdom. However, your circle is far bigger; your edges of the circle touch a lot more area so you are smart enough to realize that you don't know a lot. And in most cases your child's little circle resides inside your circle because you have been "down that road before."

Now back to the other Circle of Influence and the Square of Life. As the Square of Life grows for your child, so does the Circle of Wisdom, and as a result, your Circle of Influence either gets smaller or gets smaller relative to the child's Square of Life. This is because now he is beginning to realize that at times their Circle of Wisdom, although smaller than your Circle of Wisdom, may exceed some of your circle's boundaries.

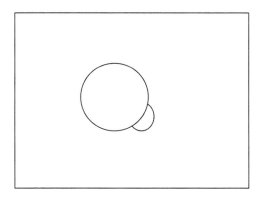

Simply put, he does not know as much as you, but some of the things he does know are different than you and this makes him all of the sudden have all the answers to life. Additionally, he has other Circles of Influence in his life: friends, girlfriends, teachers, Pastors, kids on his teams, drug dealers, thieves, cheats, and swindlers. Not only does he now have all these circles, yours is getting smaller, and these other Circles of Influence are having input on his Circle of Wisdom. Even more, these new circles are interesting to him because by now he has been listening to you for over a decade. These new people are more interesting because they are broadening his circle into areas you may not even have known he was interested in or areas you are not ready to let him go. So your teenager now wonders, "What else is Dad hiding from me?" This makes for a completely convoluted teenager. Yep, it is enough to drive you to drink for sure.

At this point, for your child's safety, you attempt to either push out your Circle of Influence and regain control or at least keep it from shrinking even more. So you push; and when your teenager sees the amount of control increase, he pushes back twice as hard. Two reasons explain this response. First of all, remember that teenagers are stupid; they already know everything, and you can't teach someone who knows everything, anything. Secondly, teenagers have found how to push boundaries out and are very adverse to having them collapse back in.

Generally what happens is that parents lose their children during the teenage years until such time as the teenager gets burned or hurt so many times that his Circle of Wisdom enlarges and he finally realizes, "Wow, Mom and Dad are right" and "I don't know everything." His Circle of Wisdom has grown to the point where the perimeter of the circle now touches so much he realizes just how little he knows. Congratulations, you have made it to adulthood. Now reconcile with your parents. I have heard many parents say how they lost their child during the "rebellious years," but the child has come back in his twenties and they have relationship again. Why does this have to be this way? Did they really lose the child, or merely lose the Circle of Influence? How did they lose the Circle? What finally expanded the child's Circle of Wisdom to the point they realize how much they don't know?

Well I have some very bad news for you. I don't have the answers either.

Be intentional, be engaged, be interactive. Be a Red Fox Father.

Just kidding, I have more. Here are my pointers for getting through these tough times.

Turn off the noise. Remember when I listed all the different Circles of Influence your teenager gets? Seems like a lot to listen to for somebody who doesn't have the wisdom gained from years of experience. Attempt to remove your children from situations whereby they have negative circles in their lives. In most cases you have the ability to control a great number of the influences. If not, then take your teenager on a trip. He won't go you say? Then take him somewhere they will be interested in, just dad and teenager. Don't try to expand your circle on this trip, just turn off the others for a couple days. You will get your opportunity; seize it when it happens.

RETREAT! When you attempt to expand your circle, your teenager will see it coming and push back twice as hard, which in turn shrinks your circle. Surprise him by retreating. You might find your teenager leaning into you if you were to move away slightly. I believe sometimes these children like to be pursued and if you don't they might turn to look to see where you are.

Ask questions. Remember, your teenager knows everything, so ask him instead of just telling him. If I told my daughter that her boyfriend disrespects her, that might turn her away from me. However, if I asked you this question, I am now making you think the way I want you to.

> Don't you think that if your boyfriend disrespects you
> now, it will continue when you get married?"

I assumed the disrespect was a forgone conclusion and now I have asked the all knowledgeable teenager for her thoughts. She may say 'no' but she will be forced to think about it. She may argue the disrespect point but now you have conversation she is interested in talking about.

> "Don't you think that if you drink and drive, chances
> are high you will eventually wreck?"

Really I am still saying 'don't you think", but without pushing my circle, now your teenager has to do something they don't generally do, think. He doesn't think because he already knows everything, when you ask him to think he find themselves in a quandary because he now realizes that he never really thought about it. When you tell him your opinion, no thinking engages, the simple answer is to disagree with dad. When you ask questions like these, he may answer your question "no" but at this point it is only to save face, they know the correct answer and they arrived at themselves and better yet you were not the one who told him what to do, you asked him what he thought. Now your teenager hears your interest in his thoughts. If they do respond no, ask him why. Again, you are making him think and a thinking teenager is a good thing. He surely isn't going to listen to your direction, comments or statements, so your only tool is to ask him to think, don't you think? See the stroke of genius here?

Introduce a Circle of Influence in his life. You pick a friend who has gone through a similar experience to what your teenager is facing. Spend some time with him and let him bring up the nasty consequences of poor decisions. Your teenager doesn't want to listen to you because you have been saying the same thing for over a decade. New circles are interesting to teenagers; bring one to the table. For example, I have a friend whose son was smoking pot. Innocent enough right? One day a police officer pulled him over, and the teenager got nervous because he had pot in the car. When the officer got close to the car, my friend's son took off. Unbeknownst to our pot smoker, the officer got caught in the rear wheel well of the car and was drugged by the car to his death. This young man has 30 years in jail to think about it. He was convicted of involuntary manslaughter and will be released from jail in his forties with no wife, no kids, no education, no experience, no money. If you don't know of a horrible story like this, find one, they are all over the place. Help expand your child's Circle of Wisdom, show them some of the consequences others have to endure for similar decisions. Introduce a third-party Circle of Influence.

I realize that teenagers are like snowflakes, no two are alike, but just like all snowflakes are cold, all teenagers are stupid. I know this because I was a teenager once and I am willing to bet you were too. The minute teenagers assume they know everything they become stupid. Most likely it is going to happen. You can't fight it, but you can contain it. If you do, you can get your teenager to adulthood having made only a couple stupid decisions, at which point he will become as wise as you and realize how much he doesn't know.

Be intentional, be engaged, be interactive. Be a Red Fox Father.

THIS IS MY TIMELINE

I don't think for a minute that my seven-year-old son ever thinks about what life is going to be like when he is eight, much less twenty or thirty. Nobody can convince me that teenagers spend much time considering what life is going to be like for them when they are twenty, thirty, or forty. I do believe that children, no matter what age, only seriously consider the here and now. These beliefs are confirmed when you see the decisions that young people make. They appear to not have much consideration for the future. A seven-year-old might be able to get away with this lack of concern for the future, but the older you get, the more important the decision becomes and more severe are the consequences. I have spoken to many young people in their late teens and early twenties and successfully introduced them to their timeline. I have seen many young people change their lives with this simple realization: there is a future *You,* that will pay the price for the *You*, you are today.

The theory is that each year a version of *You* only lives for a year and then the new you takes over and lives out the next year. For example, the twenty-year-old you only lasts for one year, and then he is done. This is the point where the twenty-one-year old you takes over. The next year, twenty-two-year old you exists, and twenty-one-year old you ceases to exist, leaving behind the circumstances, bad or good, for the new you to deal with. This goes on for numerous years until the last you takes over and no more yous follow. After forty-four years of being me, according to my outlook, there have been forty-three other Davids, and each David has laid the foundation for the David I am today. Not only are all the other Davids responsible for the David I am today, they are also responsible for the position and situation that today's David finds himself in. Next May 30, the forty-fifth David will take over, and his starting point will be where David forty-four left off. David forty-four had 365 days to take me from where David forty-three left off before handing off the position, situation and circumstances to David forty-five. For example, from some personal things that happened in my life, David number twenty-four had to pay a tough price for some decisions that David number twenty-one made. David twenty-one was not real bright and this has made all the other Davids angry; however we have forgiven him. This Fathers, I refer to as "The Timeline."

Currently, at forty-four years old, I carry a responsibility for all the other Davids to come: to fix all the problems the previous Davids have created and to better the position for all the future Davids to come. Adults usually understand this relationship exists. They may not comprehend to this specificity, but most realize that decisions and actions now affect the future and that we endure the mistakes and pay for the consequences of the past. The Timeline is a concept that most children don't understand but the sooner they do, the sooner they start making better decisions.

Let's pretend you are a seventeen-year-old boy and take a moment to look at the Timeline graphically. For the sake of easy math let's also assume you are going to live to be 100 years old.

You				
0	25	50	75	100

When you are seventeen years down this line, you still have a great distance to travel. One day you will be twenty-five, fifty, even seventy-five years old, and every number in between. The concept you must understand is that some of the decisions that the seventeen-year-old you enjoy, will have to be paid for by the twenty-five-year-old you. Furthermore, when the twenty-five-year-old you takes control of your life from the twenty-four-year-old you, he will begin with the situation that some of your decisions today have put him in along with all the decisions that each you in between has made. At this point, he will either be able to reap the benefits of great decisions all the prior yous have made or the twenty-five-year-old you will struggle in order to overcome all the poor decisions that you have made, some of which you are making now. Then comes the twenty-six-year-old you. At twenty-six, you will either reap or endure all the decisions that the prior yous have made, especially those that the twenty-five-year-old you has made. At seventeen you are most likely struggling with the possibility of drug and alcohol abuse, sex, education, which college to attend, and so on and so forth. With each decision you must consider what the future yous are going to think of past you. Let's say that the seventeen-year-old you decides to do illegal drugs, and this causes some health problems and a criminal record. Look down the Timeline.

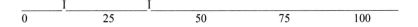

	I		I		
0		25		50	75	100

You get to pay the price for this poor decision for a long time relative to the time you have already lived. There are going to be a lot of future yous who are going to be very unhappy as they endure the consequences of your decisions today. For example, the thirty-year-old you will have to find a job, and with a criminal record the seventeen-year-old you has limited your options. The consequences of the choices you make today will be felt even thirteen years later!

One day you might want to get married, and the decisions regarding sex that you are making today will not only affect all the future yous, but also some young lady out there who will pay the price for these decisions. Twenty-five percent of teens have a sexually transmitted disease, and they will live with this through the rest of their Timeline. Also remember that this young lady has a Timeline of her own, and until your Timeline intersects with hers, she is facing similar decisions.

You don't seem to be applying yourself at school. Let's look at the Timeline one more time.

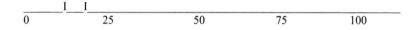

Because of your age, your mother and I are only going to support you for a little more time. At this point, the twenty-two-year-old you will have to find a full-time job, a place to live, and a car to drive and be ready to lay the foundation for all the remaining seventy-eight yous yet to live. These are important times, and if you would like seventy-eight more yous to have to struggle because you don't feel like applying yourself in school now, then it will be a price seventy-eight other yous will have to pay. However, the seventeen-year-old you only has 365 days to properly position all future yous, and this is not a long time to have to ask one you to focus.

Red Fox Fathers, I truly believe that the one problem with teenagers is that nobody gives them a specific and detailed picture what their future looks like and tells them that they will be held accountable for it. I think they get speeches and lectures on the future, and they know that it exists, but they never see just how much time it is graphically and on paper. They don't understand that they will have to endure or reap the benefits from the decisions they make today; it is a concept they just can't seem to get their young minds wrapped around. They get overwhelmed by the here and now because the here and now are overwhelming. However, if you can get your teen to focus on the future, I believe that you will have a teen more concerned with the decisions he or she is making today. I think that teens don't mind letting themselves or their parents down, but when they actually come to the realization that there is some person out there . . . *them*, who will eventually have to dig themselves out of the hole they have put their future selves into, they might be more thoughtful about the decisions they are making today. Also remember that the future you will pay the price for not being an intentional and engaged father today. Don't let *you* down.

Be intentional, be engaged, be interactive. Be a Red Fox Father.

ADRIFT

I like to vacation on the beaches of Destin, Florida. When I first started going there it, was a small beach town without much shopping or restaurants. I liked it that way. Although those days are over for Destin, I can't help but continue to vacation there. The crowds are large and there is a plethora of shopping and restaurants, yet I am still drawn like a moth to a flame. Not only is the town crowded these days, but our drive is eight hours on mapquest, or about eleven hours in real time with three small children. I actually like the long drive because it gives my wife and me some time together and because the kids are trapped and forced to talk to us. I am one of those dads that shuts off the movie in the car and makes the kids play some old-fashioned traveling games.

On our last visit to Destin, I was with my six-year-old daughter, four-year-old son, and my brand new baby girl, all on a beach with thousands of other parents with their little ducklings as well. I didn't say a thousand other fathers because many of the moms were there by themselves with children. The dads were playing golf, I would later find out. On this particular day the beach was packed, and children were all over the place. I was keeping a sharp eye on my two older ones while my wife was tending to the needs of our infant. Although it is the Gulf of Mexico, the waves were pounding the shore fairly significantly, and the tide had brought miles of seaweed. My children and I were in negotiations over our next sandcastle development when I heard a mother call out to her son, "Jason, Jason, oh my God, Jason!" My wife popped up in attempt to find out what was going on. Apparently, Jason was lost.

During college, I took a class on being a lifeguard and was instructed if you ever lose a child near the water to always check the water first. So, with that training I headed out to sea. People were gathering on the beach and began to look for little Jason. About five-years-old, red bathing suit, green surf shirt. Luckily for Jason, he had a twin, so we knew exactly who we were looking for. As I walked through the water, waist deep in sea-weed, I imagined the worst. The ocean vast, the current tough, and the water filled with sea-weed, I couldn't even see my knees. What about sharks, jellyfish or other dangerous sea creatures? My hope was that Jason merely got distracted while he was playing, slowly drifted down the coast a bit, and was still playing in the relative safety of the surf.

I also found myself getting quite angry. What was this woman doing that was so important to not pay attention to two five-year-olds when the beach was so crowded and the ocean so dangerous. Surely she could have found the time to check on her kids from time to time, adjust their course, direct them away from danger, keep them from becoming adrift. Shouldn't this be her first priority?

Adrift. I think that all our children have a tendency to find themselves there. Now I am not speaking of physically being in the current and just floating somewhere at the mercy of water. I am speaking adrift as in just floating somewhere at the mercy of life, distracted by the unknown, interesting, or even dangerous, and being tossed around by the strong current of peer pressure. This lady who lost her child knew the water was there, knew the current was strong, and knew the beach was crowded, but she let herself get distracted by her cell phone, *People* magazine, a good book, or friends. Meanwhile she lost the most important thing, her child. She might have even gotten tired of constantly being on guard. Often times I have been to the pool with my three children and have found that I am completely worn out afterwards. I feel as if I am on constant alert looking for my children. At times I even count them: one, two, three. Yep they're all here. Then, two minutes later, one, two, three. Yep they're all here. You can imagine how this gets tiring when we are at the pool.

This mom got lucky and eventually found Jason, but not all moms are this lucky. This story could have had a completely different ending. When Jason wandered off, this mom had no idea if the child was going someplace safe or going to become adrift in a large ocean. She should have stayed close and provided constant guidance. Even though Jason may not have understood the dangers out there and may have gotten tired of the constant intervention, it is our job to stay the course and keep our children from wandering off in dangerous waters or even getting caught up by the waves of peer pressure.

Red Fox Fathers, I would submit to you that we have to be on alert even when we are not at the beach. There is always something lurking around the corner to sweep up our children or have them go with the current, until one day they are lost, completely adrift, in a sea of people with other priorities, other concerns, who are even adrift themselves. It's your job, dad, to stay alert, to put down the magazine. One, two, three. Yep, they're all here.

Be intentional, be engaged, be interactive, be alert. Be a Red Fox Father.

CLEAN UP ON AISLE 9

Occasionally my wife gives me the unfortunate task of picking up a few things at the grocery store. I realize that this sounds innocent, but for some reason once I get in the grocery store, I am totally lost. I totally lose confidence in my ability to do anything at this point because I am out of control, confused, dazed, and bewildered. Usually it is only a "few items" that she wants me to pick up, but the problem is that those few items come in about 6,000 different sizes, flavors, quantities, and varieties. So when you take a few items, let's say three, and multiply it by the aforementioned sizes, flavors, quantities, and varieties, you end up with about 18,000 items I have to go through to get to the three items that I was originally intended to fetch. So there I am, dazed, confused, and frustrated, wandering around like an old man in a park looking for his newspaper, even at times forgetting why I even came to the grocery store to begin with. Finally, I call my wife (thank God for cell phones) and say "honey, just text me what I am supposed to get." Rarely, very rarely, does anybody come up to me and proactively offer help, and rarely do I ever bury my embarrassment to proactively ask for help. So there I am, on aisle nine, looking for the 2%, half gallon, organic milk, produced by Milroy Farms with DHA added that is in the red carton, not the blue and is actually found on the health food aisle, not the dairy aisle. Surely, you can relate to my bewilderment, as I am certain that you have had the daunting task of picking up three things from the grocery store and probably dread it as I do. After twelve years of marriage you would think that I would have a solution for all of this, yet I have nothing, absolutely nothing. Simply out of control, confused, dazed, and bewildered on aisle nine trying to buy milk.

Recently, the family and I went on a Disney vacation, the kind that you do only once every so many years because we definitely went all out. My goal for this vacation was to not worry about money, which is hard for me and my conservative nature. However, I had been working hard and wanted to experience the high life. So I left my wallet at the door, which I now understand is a requirement anyway, went to the deluxe resort, and worked really hard on getting over the money I was spending. It was at this deluxe resort when I took my kids to the concierge breakfast area while my wife was getting ready for the day. Apparently, this was some sacred room that in my previous forty something years I never knew existed because I never could afford access. I felt kind of awkward because this Special Room never allowed the regular middle class, so I was not really sure how to carry myself. I did find a way to get past that and prepare a breakfast for my three children. While we enjoyed a wonderful breakfast, I began to look at all the wealthy fathers in this Special Room. I figured that they all made a significant amount of money, had tremendous responsibility, employed many people, had their own businesses, were leaders, and they were all quite successful. After all, they were in the Special Room. One interesting thing that they all had in common was that they looked like I looked in the grocery store: out of control, confused, dazed, and bewildered. Like me, they had left their wife in the hotel room so she could get ready for the day, and these guys' confusion came not because they didn't belong in the

Special Room, but was because they had no clue what to do with their children; they were out of control. Amazingly, these wealthy business leaders were melted, broken down, distraught by their own children, most of whom were under the age of five. I watched how they aimlessly wandered around the room trying to please their children's appetite and desire for toys. I observed how the children seemed to intentionally manipulate their fathers. These fathers wandered around like old men in a park looking for their newspapers. They knew that they should know more. Given so many trips to the grocery store, they should have had a solution for this by now, but they had nothing. Their children wanted something, and dad would go fetch. Like trained little animals, these dads went to great lengths to meet their child's every little want and desire in order to see to their child's happiness. Nice motives, but it was pure chaos.

Fathers have been trained by society to believe that the definition of being a good father is to provide for our children. Can't you hear that ringing in your head? "You must provide for your family!" Off to work you go. Work gets you money, and with money you can provide. Therefore, the definition of providing is items money can buy. Of course, this not only means food and shelter, but also the things that make the family happy . . . toys! Notice when people talk about providing for the family, they don't really say what they think should be provided. Most people expect the same conclusion. When I feel pressure to provide for my family, I always like to ask one simple question: provide what? In our materialistic society, the natural conclusion a regular dad would make is to provide things, things that make them happy. However, the Red Fox Father answers this question much differently. My quest is to provide them with a relationship, confidence, and wisdom. I am providing things much more important than money can buy.

How often do we hear children of extremely wealthy Americans having drug problems, serving time in jail, or even committing suicide? Stuff is not the answer. If it were, our mission would be so much easier and so much clearer. Our solutions would be found at WalMart or Toys R Us.

Red Fox Fathers, don't be out of control, confused, dazed, and bewildered, like me in a grocery store or dads at Disney. Take control of your children no matter where, no matter when; don't wait for your wife to have to do it. While your children like to have toys for fleeting happiness, your children yearn for your leadership. While it is in their nature, and part of growing up, to push limits, it is your job to be their father first, not their friend. Just as in the grocery store, there are probably 18,000 different situations, requests, needs, and so on and on when you are a dad. Don't be like me in a grocery store, an idiot. Take this time right now to reread the Mission Statement and ask yourself what's missing and do you agree with it? Remember nowhere in the Mission Statement does it say that your job is to make your child happy. Happiness is not the product, it is a byproduct of creating confidence and teaching them to be loving, joyful, peaceful, patient and to exercise kindness, gentleness, and self-control. Let me be clear, your job is not to assure your children are happy; you have a greater calling. While I enjoy seeing my children happy, what I really desire is to teach them how to obtain joy. Consider the Chinese adage; "Give a man a fish and you feed him for a day. Teach a man to fish and you feed him for a lifetime." Give them a toy, you make them happy for a day; teach them joy, you give them something that lasts forever. Joy is everlasting.

Red Fox Fathers, you don't have to meet every want and desire of your children. Their love for you is not conditional upon what you can buy them, even if this is what they tell you. A "no" every once in a while can be healthy for your child. If you don't teach them how to be happy without, you are preparing yourself for tough teenage years when the requests are much more dangerous and permanent than toys. Focus on what you are truly creating, which is not fleeting happiness. If happiness is all your goal is you are simply out of control, confused, dazed, and bewildered, like me on asle nine. Rise to the challenge before you, a much greater challenge than merely picking up three things at the grocery store and a couple from the toy store. Dad, you have a greater calling.

Be intentional, be engaged, be interactive. Be a Red Fox Father.

ENEMY OF MY ENEMY

Your mother is so fat . . . I am sure that you have heard all these jokes. Your momma this, your momma that. The jokes and one-liners are numerous. All these things are funny, right? When I was in middle school anytime that you wanted to bring somebody to blows, all you had to do was talk about the other person's mother. If ever somebody said something bad about you, the simple reply to one up him was, "your momma." I can distinctly remember two kids standing off toe to toe and somebody saying "your momma." It was on: fists flailing, blood, black eyes; they came to blows. You could say someone's dad was unemployed, mental, fat, ugly, or even unknown to you and nothing. When you said something bad about somebody's mom, those were fighting words, and whether it was true or not, it was time to come to blows. It was so popular that MTV eventually had a contest show whereby the two contestants went toe to toe insulting each other's mother. Genius.

I also remember sitting in the car with my dad and being forced to listen to a song by Jerry Reed called "She Got the Goldmine, I Got the Shaft." I would guess I was an early teen when I watched my dad sing along with Jerry. It was a heartfelt moment for him. Me too, but I assure you, in a much different way. Jerry sang about his particular divorce and I think the title says it all. Apparently Jerry was very displeased with the way the judge split the assets and the income and he thought that he was left with the short end of the stick. The song made it sound like Jerry's ex-wife made off living in the lap of luxury while he suffered. Worse, it made me realize the anger my Dad held against my Mom and what he thought of what she supposedly did to him financially.

> She got the goldmine, (She got the goldmine,)
> I got the shaft. (I got the shaft.)
> They split it right down the middle,
> And then they give her the better half.

You can imagine as I wore the same pair of jeans to school every day and my mom sewed my shirts from scratch, I wasn't as amused as my dad by the song. Out of respect, I sat, listened, and didn't comment.

Just so that I give equal time to both parents, I distinctly remember my mother saying, "All men are bastards" up until the time I asked her, "Mom, I am becoming a man. Am I going to be a bastard, too?" She stopped saying this after my question.

As a "Child of a Broken Home," I spent much of my time stuck in the middle between my mother and some in her family speaking poorly of my dad, and my dad and some in his family speaking poorly of my mother. Overheard phone conversations, dinner with the grandparents, so on and so forth. Never once, not once, did anybody take into consideration that they were insulting MY mother, or MY father. How could this have been overlooked? How did they not understand that children determine their identity by who they believe their parents to be? How did they not understand that society defines children by impressions of their parents? Don't believe me? Let me tell you of a recent conversation I had with a father. He came to me worried that his daughter was going to marry a "Child of a Broken Home." The ironic thing was this man was divorced and had himself created some Children of a Broken Home. Ironic, right? Not to me. He sat in front of me and actually wondered if this young man was going to take care of his daughter and questioned his commitment all because this young man's parents were divorced. He identified this suitor by who he thought this man's parents were. What I wanted to say, I stumbled on verbally. Below is the email.

*This is his **only** shot to recapture what was lost to him as a child: a solid home with an active, engaged father and husband. Only this time he enters into it as the father/husband, and he has a little more control. This thirst, the thirst for a stable family life, that he carries has to be quenched, and I would bet you that he completely understands that this is his only shot at it and is very determined to be successful. So much so that he will be more intentional about his relationship with his wife and your daughter. The worst thing that anybody can say to him right now is "You're nothing more than your dad." My bet is this would bring him to a fight, physically. He does not want to be labeled that. The burden he carries is he has to prove to himself and everybody else that he is not his father, and this is larger than life for him. I would also expect that he holds his mother in very high regard for raising him by herself. If anything, your daughter might find herself jealous from time to time regarding the respect he has for his mother. She should be so lucky. As time goes on, it will most likely transfer to your daughter once children are on the scene.*

Not to say that things won't be tough from time to time. You and I both know they will. I would think, though, that he will be driven to see things through. He has a special motivator that he wakes up with every single morning that many people don't have, and it's that "this won't happen to me, again."

You find some of your identity by who your parents are. Even at a young age I was aware that divorce brings with it a great deal of hurt between the parties. Not just broken hearts and destroyed dreams, but also a complete destruction and division of the assets with additional expense related to having the same income now supporting the same number of people but with two households. What I never understood is why the parents take a situation that is bad for them and multiply the hurt and drag the children into the mud, thereby making it tough for them to seek and attain their dreams. Having a parent leave the house and become less part of your life is a confidence buster; no matter what others say, it is still rejection and nothing is the same. I heard numerous times growing up, "It has nothing to do with you," which begs the obvious questions:

> Then why does it hurt so much?
> Why do you keep dragging me back in?
> Why am I being used as a pawn?
> Why do I suffer for your financial arguments?
> Why are you insulting my mother/dad in front of me?
> Why am I now known as Child of a Broken Home?
> Why all of the sudden do I have to go to this after-school
> program full of other Children of a Broken Home?
> Why are all these kids so angry and fight so much?

If you find yourself in divorce or already have had one, understand that no matter how much you have softened the blow, no matter how much you have remained interactive, engaged, and intentional, your child will have pain. He or she may say everything is okay, it's not. I do have some good news for you, though. You purchased this book, so you care. Take to heart the things in this book. Be intentional, be interactive, and be engaged, and do it all to a fault. Just because the marriage is over doesn't mean that your relationship with your children should be. This would just add insult to injury. The relationship is your responsibility, not theirs.

If your ex-wife or her family is speaking poorly of you, all you can do is continue to prove her wrong by being a good father and not entertaining the verbal sparring, and certainly not in front of your children. If you can be the Red Fox Father, I can guarantee you, from personal experience, as your children grow older, they will have a clear vision of reality, and you will not need to defend yourself, even if, unfortunately, your children have to defend you. Children of a Broken Home have no choice. It is just one more thing on a long list of things that we shouldn't have to deal with after divorce. We defend our parents whether the attack is true or not.

I know that misery loves company, and when you are hurt, there is nothing quite like having somebody to commiserate with; the enemy of my enemy can be my friend. However, to create in your child the enemy of your wife,—well, consider what you have created. One day your child will resent you for it. Just like at my middle school, it's not wise to speak poorly of anybody's mother, most importantly your child's. Whether it's true or not, you just may find yourself coming to blows.

Be intentional, be engaged, be interactive. Be a Red Fox Father.

THE AIRPLANE

P rior to your reading this I am going to ask for your forgiveness. This one is just for me; I have to get something off my chest.

I have <u>never</u> told this story before, and nobody knows this but me. I have kept this secret for somewhere around thirty years and it's time. So this musing will most likely offer you nothing of value, but you might find the story somewhat interesting.

In his bedroom sits a little boy playing with a remote control airplane. The plane has about an eighteen inch wingspan, is silver, and is an exact duplicate of a P51 Mustang. The plane has a small gasoline propeller engine and once airborne is controlled by remote. Imagine this little boy's delight when this gift was opened Christmas morning. It was exactly what this boy wanted for Christmas. Or was it?

I am not sure how old I was, but I remember seeing a neighborhood kid with a remote control airplane. He and his dad were going to an open field on this particular day so his dad could teach him how to fly the airplane using the remote. I couldn't imagine anything that I wanted more: my dad to spend time with me flying a remote control airplane. I held on to my airplane for years doing everything I possibly could in an effort to make that stupid thing fly and to make my dad play with me. Somehow I even bought a small canister of gasoline, brought it into my room, and poured gas into the engine. I remember one day the propellers turned for about three seconds before dying out. That was a great day, so much so I remember it thirty years later. I am not sure what I would have done had the engine started, and I don't have the slightest idea how I managed to get gasoline in my room. I even spilled some at one point onto the carpet, but I didn't care. I had a remote control airplane, and my dad was supposed to show me how to fly it. He never did, and it never flew. I sat in my room and flew that plane in my mind's eye, holding the base of the plane with my hand. I made engine noises and jumped on the bed and then crawled on the floor, but the plane never took a solo flight.

I kept that plane for years collecting dust on my shelf. The plane and I patiently waiting for my dad to come by and show us how to take flight, then it happened. As I grew older, I remembered the real reason why I wanted the plane in the first place. I didn't need another toy; I needed a toy that my dad had to show me how to use. It was never about the plane, it was about time with my dad. Eventually I pulled the plane off the shelf and realizing that the purpose for the plane would never be fulfilled and that all the plane did was bring back yet another disappointment and horrible memories of unmet expectations. This was the day that the plane would make its initial and final flight. It flew outside under the power of my hand, and I threw it away. It never served its purpose.

Red Fox Fathers, you may never understand why your children sometimes behave the way they do or want some of the things they want, and maybe they don't, either, but I can tell you from personal experience that every child has a little something inside of him deep down in his heart that makes him seek time with you that seeks your approval, and a connection with you. A child may not even like the fact that this need exists, but it does, and it can make a child do frustrating things, act out, or buy stupid things. So when your child is acting out, take the time to reflect. Is he merely seeking time with you? It is worth contemplating, and it's worth acting on. Dad, worse case scenario is that you spend time with your child. So feel free to err on the side of being right no matter what the child's motive. Don't leave your child thirty years later having a memory of a plane engine running for three seconds as a highlight in your relationship.

Be intentional, be engaged, be interactive. Be a Red Fox Father.

FOR PETE'S SAKE

Shortly after we purchased our home, I met Pete. He was about eight years old when I first met him, and he often came from several houses down the street when I was outside playing with my own children. Being the type of father who is careful about my children's playmates, I made sure to introduce myself to Pete right away. Pete was a couple of years older than my children, so I just wanted to be certain that he was going to be a good kid for my kids to play with. I observed how Pete paid special attention when he was around the younger children taking their feelings and needs into consideration. Pete was a kind and thoughtful young man, and I let him play with us whenever he saw us outside.

One time when it was pouring rain in the summer time, my kids wanted to play in the rain, so outside we went, and Pete somehow joined us. He was probably looking out his window wishing he could come down the street to play when he saw us in the pouring rain running around like crazy people. We actually walked down to the lake that had created a small river, and Pete and my kids rode their bikes through it. Plain and simple, Pete was a good kid. Being the type of father that I am, I often wondered why Pete's dad didn't seem to spend much time with him. His dad's car was in the driveway and Pete was outside, but his father was nowhere to be found. I wondered how Pete could be such a good boy when his dad didn't seem to play with him too much. I simply conceded that I was unaware of what went on inside the home and that maybe Pete's dad was an indoor Red Fox Father. But still, I was curious. I know that I only have a short time with my children, so I try to make the most out of it, indoors and out.

As time went on, I saw Pete less and less, but I did notice that Pete and his dad were now playing outside together. It was no longer strange to see Pete and his dad riding their bikes down the street or throwing the ball in the yard. I found this additionally curious because it seemed kind of all the sudden that Pete's dad began to engage. I didn't think much of it, but I was happy for Pete that this additional time was being afforded him. One sunny weekend I saw Pete and his dad outside together when I mentioned to my wife, "Have you noticed that Pete and his dad hang out together now?" Obviously, my curiosity lingered. "Oh," she said, "I forgot to tell you Pete's dad has been diagnosed with a terminal illness."

My heart completely sank into my stomach. Terminal illness, Pete's dad was only a little bit older than I and Pete is only a little bit older than my children! Then it occurred to me that the explanation for Pete and his dad spending more time together was that his dad had been given two years to live. Seems reasonable to most after all, that is most likely what all of us would do but I actually found myself a little angry too. The Red Fox Father in me considered what would have happened had Pete's dad not gotten that diagnosis. Would he still have engaged with his child or just let him grow up without an intentional relationship with his son? What if Pete's dad's death was not given a time? What if his terminal illness was all of the sudden? Now, he had a date.

Not a good one, mind you, but he had time to make up for all the years when he thought that his largest contribution would be his work. Things had been put in perspective for Pete's dad, and now, with only months left, he realized all the time wasted and how precious the remaining time was. Apparently, number one on his bucket list is "spend more time with Pete."

Red Fox Fathers, I have to give you some tough news for you to hear. News I want you to take very seriously and never forget. Like Pete's dad, you're dying, too, and there is only a little time left. The difference between us and Pete's dad is Pete's dad had the date. He knew what his future held, and he had taken action. Pete's dad had the wakeup call and began to value the things most important to him, Pete. I bet Pete's dad watched less TV and argues less with his wife over little things. I know for certain that Pete's dad spent more time with Pete, inside and outside the house. Pete's dad lived out the rest of his life as if he was dying because he knew he was. Your prognosis is a little different from Pete's dad's. You (I hope) have more time than he did and you most likely are completely unaware of how much time you have left. It could be more, but it could be less. The end result is the same though, the diagnosis is grim: you're dying, dad. We all are.

There are several different ways you can react to this news you just received. You could go skydiving, rocky mountain climbing, or 2.7 seconds on a bull named Fu Man Chu. Or you could do what Pete's dad did: get engaged, be intentional, and don't take these final few years, months, or days for granted. I still don't know if Pete knows of the situation with his dad but Pete does know that all of a sudden his dad is engaged, intentional, and interactive and after Pete's dad passes I have to consider if Pete is going to wonder why his dad didn't engage earlier. What are your children going to think about you after your time is spent?

Red Fox Fathers, for Pete's sake, get in the game! Live as if you are dying! The truth is you are.

Be intentional, be engaged, be interactive. Be a Red Fox Father.

CHANCES ARE

Chances are slim that you will be killed by falling space debris. Actually they are about one in five billion still possible, but not probable. Chances of death by freezing, one in three million. How about a lightning strike? One in two million. Chances of being killed by a dog, one in 700,000. A tornado has a one in two million chance of killing you and a shark, one in sixty-five million, so give some respect to the tornado beating out the shark. I generally don't like to leave things to chance. Although there is not much I can do about falling space debris, some things I do to help with my chances are that I don't tend to climb into freezers or take long walks in snowstorms. I also go inside during thunderstorms, or during tornado warnings, and, of course, I don't mill about in shark-infested waters.

Gambling is a game of chance, especially the roulette wheel. A little game with a wheel that has a bunch of numbers and three colors, red, black, and green. With every spin of the wheel a ball bounces around and eventually lands in one of the numbered and colored slots. I will concede that I have spent time sitting at a roulette wheel thinking that if I bet on black after it hits red, I have a greater chance of winning, but the accountant in me knows that each spin black has the same exact chance of hitting as it did the time before, no more, no less. The wheel doesn't care what color it landed on the time before; each spin stands on its own. I don't bet on green because although the payout is good, the chances of hitting one of the green slots is about 5%. It just doesn't do it for me. The actual chances of hitting black are somewhere around 47%.

Life is full of chance. What are the chances that somebody will run a red light while I have green? Sometimes I wonder if the person driving the other direction on a two-lane road is texting; I bet the chances are high. The worst thing about chance is that I find that I seem to leave some important things to chance. For example, I have a tendency to leave the relationship with my wife to chance. I work all day, come home, take care of the children, help with homework, coach baseball, take care of the house and the household finances, work some more, then watch Sportscenter and the day is done. My relationship with my wife? There is a chance that it is as good as it was the day we got married, but there is also a chance that it is not.

Recently I have heard of numerous couples who have gotten to the point that they feel as if their marriage has become more like roommates. They share the same home, equally love the children, and share the same goals, but the desire to be with one another forever is just gone. Actually, they just dread the thought. It makes you wonder, what happened? At one time this man looked into this woman's eyes and thought, "I just can't live without her." Fast forward ten years and all they are trying to do is get the kids out of the house so they can divorce and start their lives again. I would submit to you they left their relationship to chance. I think that when you leave your relationships to chance, life can be a cruel roulette wheel; like betting on green, it just won't do it for you.

Life's demands leave you no time to live your life. You get caught up in a whirlwind of keeping up with the Joneses, never realizing the Jones Family is on a path to divorce and whose children will soon find themselves ill equipped to handle the demands of life. Rinse and repeat. Like a gambler who gets caught up in the whirlwind of gambling, sitting there down hundreds of dollars thinking, "If I just bet more, I can win it all back." The beat goes on.

So, dad, here you are, sitting at a roulette wheel betting on green, down a couple hundred, thinking "I just need to keep doing this, and I can dig myself out of this." Dad, you are standing in a bucket trying to lift yourself up by the handle; it's just not going to do it for you. It is hard to accept your losses, but they exist whether you accept them or not. The only thing that you can control is your future because the past doesn't give a darn about you, and dwelling on it only steals your future. What you can do is not bet on green, not leave things to chance. Get intentional, quit worrying about the Joneses, quit working so much, manage your time, make an effort to spend time with your wife, and, dare I say it, turn off Sportscenter. Get to know your wife like you did when you were dating. It might surprise you to find out who she has become.

I have some more interesting statistics for you. About 14% of sexually active girls attempt suicide compared to only 5% of those not sexually active. That seems to be about three times as many. Twenty-five percent of sexually active teens are depressed versus 7.7% of teens who are not sexually active. One in two sexually active teenagers will contract an STD by the age of twenty-five. Over 60 % of teenagers say they know drugs are kept, sold, and used at their school. Sixty-three percent of teenagers who drink say they got the alcohol from their friend's house. Twenty five percent of teenagers have used an illicit drug in the past thirty days; over 37 % have used in the last year.

You can see there is a good chance that your child will one day engage in premature sexual activity or illicit drug use. Do you ever wonder what is the difference between those children who do and those children who don't? I wonder what the difference would be if you put all the fathers in a room whose kids didn't do drugs and in another room you put the fathers whose kids did do drugs. Dad, I am telling you one group didn't leave it to chance. One group was intentional, one group was engaged, one group was interactive. These dads may not have kept up with the Joneses but they didn't just sit at the roulette wheel of life and allow their children to bounce around from place to place hoping they'd land by chance in the green, a 5% chance.

Be intentional, be engaged, be interactive. Be a Red Fox Father.

SHOW ME YOUR FRIENDS

I was completely surprised when Jay told me that he had to leave work because of his son's court date. Jay had worked for me for a couple years now and was a great employee, dedicated, organized, committed, and very good at his responsibilities. I knew Jay had several children, and one of them even worked in another department. Par for the course, she was a competent, reliable employee as well. I didn't know his other children personally, but it is a small town, and his children were always good kids. So you could imagine my surprise when Jay needed time off for a court date. Jay was surprised, too.

Jay received a call late one night that his son had been caught engaged in vandalism. Good thing for Jay and his son that this boy had never been in such trouble before. Trouble? His son had never been in any trouble until now. Jay went on to tell me how his son met Derrick at school. Derrick had been in trouble before, and his son was getting involved in activities that Jay had been able to keep his other children from. Jay completely laid the blame for his son's newfound behavior on Derrick, understandably so as Derrick was quite experienced with the law. So off to court Jay went and returned with some good news, another chance from the judge. Jay's boy got off with some community service and a slap on the hand.

Now that I think about it, I guess I shouldn't have been so surprised about the news of the court date. I guess after the description of Jay and family I should have been, but I wasn't. No, no, no, I don't mean the first court date of course that one was a complete surprise. I am referring to the second court date. Jay came to me a few weeks later to request more time off for another court date. Apparently, Derrick decided to up the ante and proceeded to commit a burglary while armed with a 9mm Ruger. Derrick was not the kind of kid who liked to do things alone, so who else but Jay's kid to go with him? After all, misery loves company.

Now I was not sure who Derrick's dad was, but I knew Jay's son's father, and he was definitely the type of dad who taught his son to know the difference between right and wrong and also instructed him in the benefits of making correct choices. The problem was that even with years of instruction and learning, Jay could not overcome the power of peer pressure. While the decision to commit armed robbery was being pondered by Derrick and Jay's son, Derrick was there, but Jay was not. So Derrick, who had not been taught the value of doing the right things, played to Jay's son's emotions, countering the instruction Jay's son had received, but with no rebuttal available from Jay. With gun in hand, Derrick began the perfect crime and broke into a home in his own neighborhood while everybody was at work, or so he thought. A neighbor watched from a window in a nearby house, and now Jay had to stand before the Judge trying to explain, "It's not my kid, it's Derrick." But this time the judge just didn't buy it. Most likely because it was not Derrick's fault nor Jay's son's fault; the truth is; it's Jay's.

I can hear you saying it, "But David, Jay did all the right things!"
Did he now? Jay was aware of the overwhelming influence of
Derrick, and he also knew Derrick had not been taught the ability
to make wise decisions. I would submit to you that Jay should
have gotten Derrick out of his son's life, no matter how difficult it
might have been. Had Jay removed Derrick from influencing his
son, Jay would not have had to stand in court trying to explain
why his son got in trouble . . . the second time.

Red Fox Fathers, I think that it is an unwritten law of the world
that if you add good plus bad, you don't get good, you don't get
average, you simply get bad. Don't believe me? Literally, put a
bad apple in a basket with other apples. You won't end up with a
basket of average apples. You see, it was impossible for Jay's son
to influence Derrick for good: it goes against the laws. Nor was it
possible even to land these two boys on average. Derrick dragged
Jay's good son down to bad: the laws of nature were in Derrick's
favor. If I we're to stand on a chair, and you were to stand on the
ground, it is far easier for you to pull me down than it would be
for me to pull you up. There is no middle ground; either I go down
or you go up. I am sure it is easy for you to see how no matter
who is standing in the chair, the guy on the ground always has
the advantage.

There are those who would say that Jay's son did the right thing
by maintaining the relationship with Derrick in order to try to
lift Derrick up and have a positive impact on his life. However, let
me propose this: At what risk do you do this? After all, Derrick's
parents were not able to accomplish this, and certainly his teachers
tried unsuccesfully. Now Jay is going to think that his son has the
unique strength and ability to save this boy from sixteen years of
bad decisions, lack of wisdom, and general neglect. Not likely.

What Jay didn't realize was that Derrick was not going to become Jay's son; Jay's son was going to become Derrick.

There are about a million quotations out there that relate to business that tell us the importance of surrounding ourselves with good people, the best people, yet we expect our children to go out there and make a difference in somebody's life by being able to influence another for good. When I hire people, I do my due diligence. I have three people interview them, I perform a background check, check references, I drug test them and I do whatever else I can to make sure that I have a top notch employee; the company's future is at stake here. Yet we allow our teenagers to create relationships without as much as a Q and A session. Shame on us.

Our mantra should be simple, "Show me your friends and I will tell you your future". Your children will be influenced by their friends; it is going to happen. Fathers, you have the line item veto power here to remove people from your children's lives, don't be shy, use it. You don't need a crystal ball to find out if your kids are going to do drugs, engage in crime, etc. Look deep into the eyes of their friends, perform an interview, check references, call other parents and teachers, do your due diligence. Make sure that your child has a top notch friend. Your child's future is at stake here.

Show me your friends, and I will tell you your future. Even at your age, Dad, it applies. Who are you hanging out with?

Be intentional, be engaged, be interactive. Be a Red Fox Father. Be with other Red Fox Fathers.

SAVING PRIVATE RYAN

The M16's barrel was still hot to the touch. Private Ryan squatted down behind the destroyed truck, panting from his recent advancement against the enemy. The heat of the desert was thick, and everything was covered in sand, even Private Ryan. Private Ryan checked his ammo, sidearm, and remaining grenades and then blew the sand out of the dangerous parts of his rifle. He noticed that his thumbs and index finger were growing blisters. The enemy was relentless and outnumbered Private Ryan and his comrades; Private Ryan had already witnessed in graphic detail two soldiers from his unit go down. One took a fatal wound during battle, and the other received sniper fire to the head. I will spare you the gory detail that Private Ryan saw but you can let your mind wonder.

After three hours of intense battle, the good guys were finally advancing. The insurgents had taken hold of Faluja weeks ago but faced with the force of the US military they finally retreated to a well-fortified compound. This attack had been planned for some time, and Private Ryan was confident and very familiar with the compound, including its ten foot walls laced with barbed wire, security cameras, and small mine field. Numerous holes in the walls had been created to distribute enemy sniper fire. Private

Ryan surveyed the compound and quickly ducked back down in his hidden position. He took a moment to grab another handful of Cheetos, these being the fuel of choice for this particular military advancement, cheetos and coke that is. Finally, Private Ryan's dad arrived on the battlefield, and together they were ready to advance. Private Ryan was more familiar with the mission and began to secure the compound. Forgoing the usual call for air support, Private Ryan decided to take the compound. The thrill of the battle was what Private Ryan wanted; he was addicted to the adrenaline. The odd thing about this entire story is not just the cheetos, or that Private Ryan was fighting with his dad; it's the fact that Ryan was only six years old.

Ryan was at my coach pitch baseball practice when he relayed the story of his vast military experience. I was trying to teach Ryan some physical coordination; you know, the usual, how to get a step on a ground ball, accurately throw a baseball, and see to the timing of connecting a moving bat with a moving baseball. The fact that Ryan was behind the other children in regards to his abilities dumbfounded his father. "He is great at Halo," he claimed with overwhelming pride. For those of you that don't know, Halo is a graphic military type video game. Red Fox Fathers, I remained silent, but I had plenty to say. Ryan was overweight when we met and apparently well versed in Halo, but I could tell that he had little or no muscle, coordination, control, or even desire; his mind was on the battlefield, completely addicted. Isn't it odd how we look down on other cultures that arm their children for war and yet we let ours play video games with such life-like graphics? I am sure that Ryan had unusual Xbox skills and that his aforementioned blistered thumb and index finger were straight wired to his brain, but Ryan could not grip a baseball bat, move to get in front of a baseball, or even offer his frustrated coach the ability to move a glove in front of thrown baseball. Don't get me wrong Fathers, I don't believe that my children or any member of my team will make a career from baseball; however, I do think that baseball teaches more than Halo ever could. Real life kid baseball that is, not computer games.

I distinctly remember this little boy describing his favorite game in detail. So many megapixel graphics, fifty-something-inch flat screen TV, and crisp surround sound completed with a sub woofer. Red Fox Fathers, it's okay to tell your children they have to limit computer play. Let them know there is a game out there with better graphics that are hi def and come in 3D, with surround sound and real consequences. "3D game!" Ryan exclaimed. "Yeah, Ryan, it's called outside. This ball is going to look like it's coming right at you. Here catch." Numerous times Ryan suffered the real consequences of failure with my 3D game, and in the end Ryan left the season lacking the ability to succeed in the real world. In the real world there is no reset button; more coordination is required than a blistered thumb and index finger. In the real world you only get one life.

I eventually had to excuse Ryan's father from baseball practice as his frustration with his son bubbled over, prompting Dad to use foul language during my baseball practice. I wondered why Dad was not more frustrated with himself, though. He was the one who required nothing more of Ryan than to know the difference between an M16 and an AK47. At one point during practice, Ryan and another player had a disagreement, and Ryan stated, "I will kill you!" I don't think for a minute that he actually meant what we know of the definition of kill because in the reality that Ryan spent most of his time, killing someone was a temporary situation, a mere fifteen second delay in game play. I gave Ryan special attention throughout the three month baseball season working on his coordination and trying to build some physical abilities and conditioning, but I am sure that once baseball season ended, he retreated to his comfortable chair, cool air conditioner, and the safety of his living room while he engaged in graphic violence, developing his thumb and index finger and a unique de sensitivity to violence and the loss of life. I will concede that I was fighting an uphill battle (no pun intended) as my game was in the heat of South Georgia. My game was difficult, took practice, work, discipline, and relied on teamwork. My game took some qualities that Ryan's father refused to teach him, and I could never get Ryan to understand the glory of real victory over a real opponent, with only one life to do it in.

Red Fox Fathers, challenge your children. Expose them to different things and have them master something. Teach them that practice does make perfect. Allow them to experience and obtain the joy and confidence that come from accomplishments. Lastly, help them understand the thrill of victory, and show them how to be honorable through the agony of defeat.

Be intentional, be engaged, be interactive. Be a Red Fox Father.

PROMISE KEEPERS

One thing that I remember from my childhood is my mother always saying, "Always keep your promises". It really has more effect if you read this as an Italian woman. Try again, "Always keep your promises." She used to tell me that I needed to keep my promises because it would eventually, in real life, be my reputation. "Son," she would say, "Be a man of your word." Since she used to say this all the time. I remember thinking about how hard it actually was going to be to keep all my promises, but then she told me the secret to keeping promises. "Be careful what you promise."

Throughout my life I can list for you some very important promises that have not been kept, some in my personal life, many in my professional life. It is based on those promises that I have made some of the most important decisions in my life. When a promise was broken, it hurt. Each time somebody broke a promise I silently placed that person in a different category in my world. I lost respect for him or her, didn't trust that person, didn't really want to be around him or her anymore. I am willing to bet you feel the same way about those people who have broken promises to you.

I know that I have not kept every promise to my children. I am not just talking about the big ones, but the little ones, too. I believe that if I am on my way to work and I tell my son, "when I get home, we're going to the pool," then I just made a promise. I don't think that just because I didn't say at the end of the sentence, "I promise," means that it is any less of a promise. So if then I get home and don't take him to the pool, I have broken a promise, albeit a small promise, but a promise nonetheless. Just imagine your children, hanging on every word you speak, and you tell your child you are going to the pool. They wait all day for your return, and then you don't do it. Regardless if you say, "I promise," I assure you that your children remember what you said and will expect you to follow through, until you let them down enough so that your children never believe anything you say again. Tragic. I bet you would agree not keeping your promises is not considered good parenting.

It was hot in Atlanta. No relief to be found from a passing cloud, and the air was not moving a bit, no breeze whatsoever. It was hot. I was with my daughter at the pool. She was young, and we were just soaking, relaxing, trying to escape the heat. As we splashed around, I noticed that another father, no doubt seeking relief from the heat, had brought his son to the pool. Brantley was about four and enjoying the fun, thrills, and excitement that the pool had to offer. At times it was a little too much enjoyment; Brantley was behaving poorly. Brantley's father was just trying to get some time out with his son, and the pool was the obvious choice on this day. For the sake of conversation, let's refer to Brantley's father as Jim. Jim didn't realize before coming to the pool that he was going to have a horrible day, but he should have. Jim just wanted to go to the pool and have some good father-son time. I would guess that Jim's wife made him do this because, Red Fox Fathers, Jim was clueless; however, Brantley was not. Brantley knew that Jim was not a man of his word, not a promise keeper. Each time

Brantley's behavior was unacceptable, Jim would say something like, "Brantley, stop doing that. Do it again and you are getting out of the pool!" Promise made but then Brantley would do it again, and Jim would . . . well, promise broken. This sequence occurred over and over again. Eventually, Jim told Brantley "Do it again, and we are going home!" I heard Brantley reply, "No we're not!" I could see Jim's frustration, but he had no idea what the next fourteen years were going to look like for him. He most likely thought that Brantley would just grow out of it.

Jim was actually teaching Brantley numerous things. The first lesson, was that there are no consequences for your actions. This lesson possibly could destroy any future that Brantley has. Imagine telling Brantley at fifteen the consequences for illegal drugs. Would he care? Should he? Brantley learned that consequences are not really enforced. When Brantley breaks the law, eventually he will suffer the consequences, Brantley won't have a conscience that keeps him in check; he has learned there are no consequences. Brantley has been perfectly programmed for peer pressure because there are no consequences. Secondly, Brantley doesn't trust that his father means anything he says. If reality doesn't follow what Jim says, then how is Brantley to trust his dad when he tells him the importance to look both ways before crossing the road? Why bother listening to dad? He really doesn't mean it. Brantley isn't old enough to determine if what dad says is important. At four years old, it is all important. Third, Brantley has no respect for Jim. I submit to you that Brantley's mother has no respect for Jim, either. How could she? Jim is not a man of his word and allows a four year-old to run over him. Again, I can't even imagine the life that Jim has set up for himself when Brantley is a teenager. The worst part about it is Brantley's life choices could lead him astray, and he might not recover. Jim will shrug it off as "teenagers," never realizing he caused it all. He will find solace in many of his peers who are facing the same "stage of life" teenagers.

Red Fox Fathers, heed this warning. Be a promise keeper. If you make a statement, follow through, good or bad. I know that Jim didn't want to make Brantley sit out of the pool. He loved Brantley and wanted him to be happy, but a couple minutes out of the pool, would have taught Brantley some very important things: consequences, trust, and respect. Instead, Brantley will never believe that Jim is the Great Wizard. He will always think that Jim is just a silly old man behind the curtain who doesn't know what he is talking about. I can admit to you that I have made some promises regarding consequences for my children that I did not want to follow through with, but I did. Promise made, promise kept. When we go out, people are surprised how well behaved my children are, but their mom and I have kept our promises, and all I have to do is whisper in my son's or daughter's ear, "Your behavior is unacceptable," and they know there will be consequences should they not change their ways. At times, my children still choose poorly, but I keep my promises.

Jim needs to join promise keepers; we all do. I know it's frustrating. You, as I, struggle between making sure your child is happy and making your child behave. Our job, fathers, is not to make sure that our children are happy all the time. If you take the time right now, Red Fox Father, to keep your promises, from the ones that say, "I will take you to the pool," to the ones that say, "We are leaving the pool", your Brantley will learn consequences, trust, and respect. It won't happen overnight but keep all your promises, and you eventually will find yourself not so frustrated. I promise.

Be intentional, be engaged, be interactive. Be a Red Fox Father.

Nosce te Ipsum

O r "know thyself" to those of us not so educated. I, of course, had to look it up. I am willing to go out on a limb and guess that if you are a workaholic, I know you better than you know yourself. At the end of this reading I will let you decide if I am right or not.

Most of us when we go to our job generally like what we do. I am not saying we do what we love; that is an entirely different concept. I am merely saying that if we don't do what we love, we at least try to love what it is we do. I can tell you that when I am at work, I have confidence, and I would guess that you do too. You and I know what is expected of us, the direction is clear, we know what our day looks like, we are good at what we do, and when we do what we do well, we see the benefits and experience the reward. Whether it is financial or simply a pat on the back, it feels good. So for forty plus years we will go to work Monday through Friday, sometimes more, and we create accomplishments. Even though we call it work, it becomes comfortable for us, and we get our sense of identity by what we do there. The people there are generally nice to us. So we go to parties and talk with our friends, and all we discuss is what is going on at the office. "How is business?" we ask, or if we are just meeting somebody we ask, "What do you do?" which is another way of asking, "Who is this that I am speaking to?" The first answer out of the mouth of the other man is "I am *job title*". "I am." These are powerful words, and one must be careful about the words that follow this statement. God was so careful with the words that came after "I am" that this is all he said, "I AM!" Know thyself; it is not as easy as we think because, truth be known, we are really more than a job title. At least we should be.

Compare your feeling at work to your feelings at home. Let's recap for a moment. At work you know what is expected of you, know what to do, the people are nice, and you know how to handle most any situation. At work you are confident, welcome, master of your domain, no matter how small or big, and at work you experience the gratitude of a job well done. You can feel the reward of accomplishment even if nobody rewards you. You can feel it inside and you look back and say, "I did that."

Now, let's go home. Your house is probably different than mine, so I will only speak of my situation. I walk into the house and have no idea what has gone on there for the last couple of hours. I don't know what to do because the situation is always different. I hardly know where things are most of the time, I don't understand the rules, and I have no idea where we are in the whole process. My wife is a complete and utter mystery and my daughters are not far behind. I have no idea what bit of wisdom my son needs for that day to create the man that I want him to be; and my wife holds in some secret spot in her head (or heart, who knows) her expectations for my words and next couple of actions. The field of play continuously changes with no time outs for instant replay, and what the heck: if I were allowed to have the play reviewed, I would have been out of play reviews a long time ago. Then there is the dog. God bless the dog. Sometimes I can look at the dog, and I know he knows; he knows if I am about to be in a bad situation or if everything is okay. I think this is the real reason why the dog greets me at the door, to let me know. If the dog waits for me inside when I open the door, then all is well; however, if the dog comes out to greet me, it is his way of saying, "Let's get out of here!" The dog knows, I do not. So, in summary, at home I have no confidence. I have no plan, the people are not always nice, and rarely do I ever get the satisfaction or experience the gratitude or reward of a job well done.

All this and we don't have to wonder why we become "workaholics." Forget the word "work" for a moment. That place we go to every day in the first scenario sounds like fun compared to the second scenario, doesn't it? Combine this with the pressure of having to provide a lifestyle that your wife's friends say they have. I mean they go on nice vacations, have new cars, have nice clothes and jewelry and eat at the best places, but your wife has no idea that their family is about a month away from bankruptcy and foreclosure. I am sure that you have seen it numerous times, and if you are dumb enough to keep up with them, then you will soon find yourself in the same place, bankruptcy and foreclosure. So, here you sit at work, and you might even be reading this book at work just to avoid going home to what you don't understand. Sometimes you don't stay at work to get work done, you stay at work because you don't want to go home. Sometimes you stay because you are scared to go home. Sometimes, dare I say, you stay at work until the kids go to bed. Sometimes you stay because you need that appreciation you get when you do, all the stuff you don't get at home. The dog sits by the door awaiting a rescue because on these particular days the dog was going to go out to greet you. But you are at work, a noble place to be, a noble effort; after all, you are providing for your family and only abandoning the dog. The dog knows it's every man for himself; that's how the phrase "dog eat dog" was started.

So, workaholic dad, did I get it right? Come on, admit it, you're not a workaholic because this is what the job requires. You're a workaholic because you are scared, scared to go home, scared of the unknown that is your house, scared of not being able to understand the expectations, scared of having to have "the talk" with your teenager, or just tired of being underappreciated. Home can be uncomfortable. Do you know thyself, Dad, or did I know you a little bit better?

Then there is your wife. She really wants to understand that you have to work all the time, but she doesn't understand why. All her friend's husbands don't work so late, and when she brings this up you make excuses. You say she doesn't work such long hours; you tell her she doesn't have the responsibility that you have. She gets frustrated or angry so there is yet another reason why you would work late: avoid the angry frustrated wife. So the Circle of Chaos ensues. You work late because you feel more comfortable there. Your wife gets angry, so you work late, which makes her angry, which makes you work late. You exit the Circle of Chaos in divorce court.

Red Fox Fathers, expect more from yourself. Don't be so insecure that you have to work late to avoid the scary, uncomfortable parts of being home. Take if from a guy who still doesn't know where the pots and pans go in the kitchen and still can't comprehend the proper sorting of the laundry. Whites, delicates, colored, and reds. Don't dry my jeans, some stuff hangs dry, some stuff is set flat, oh the insanity! And don't even get me started on the proper organizational chart of the pantry. Then there is the pressure of being wrong on every judgment when it comes to child rearing. I mean how on earth can you possibly compete with this unknown oracle of wisdom called "women's intuition?" All your life you have heard that only a woman knows about certain things, so your opinions are immediately discounted on the grounds you have no oracle. What's a guy to do? Retreat. Retreat to the comfort of work where you know all, where, "I am" is defined.

I challenge you, dad, to come home from work every night you can and plug into the family. If your supervisor does not specifically require you to work late, then you are home for dinner. The wife might make some crack about it but your job is not to return fire. The more you are home, the more you will be part of the complicated puzzle and the more gratification you will find when you have good input to solve the puzzle. I know nobody talks about it much, but I do believe there is something called "Dad's Intuition." Whether it be for your daughter or your son, you have some great input they need to hear, and just because your wife may not agree with you, it is no less important because you work outside of the home a little more. So go home, dad. Greet the kids, kiss the wife, help with dinner, be there every chance you get. If you really have work to do, do it after the kids go to bed but in the interim, your job is Husband and Dad. If you get home at six pm and the kids go to be at nine pm I am only asking for three hours, and you can do anything for three hours.

Red Fox Father, question your motives for being a workaholic and ask yourself if a couple things at work can wait. Get yourself to be more timely. Prioritize better so you don't have to stay late. It is important to know thyself dad but let your children and wife know you, too, and that only comes with time. Eventually with enough time, we all will figure out how to sort laundry and know where the pots and pans are located. Along with the more important things going on in our households.

Be intentional, be engaged, be interactive, Be a Red Fox Father.

THE SNOOZE BUTTON

I am not sure who invented the snooze button. I don't think that he got much recognition, and I would guess that he most likely was an underachiever. I mean this guy set his alarm clock every night, and when the alarm went off he thought, "I just want to go back to sleep." However, shutting off the alarm and resetting the time for fifteen minutes later were just too much work. "You know, there should be a button you can push to shut off the alarm for a couple more minutes." I can see him pitching a Board of Directors, a bunch of old guys sitting around a huge oak table in leather chairs.

"Son," they'd say, "you mean that you want a button to shut off the alarm for a couple minutes?" "Why don't you just set your alarm for fifteen minutes later each night?"

"No, I need to get up at a certain time, but sometimes in the morning I decide to get a little extra sleep, you know?" The Board of Directors surely ran this young inventor off.

I honestly don't believe that at six am, when I am at some point between being unconscious and partially awake, that I am at my best to make the decision to not abide by the wisdom I held the night before when I was considering all the things that I have to accomplish tomorrow.

So in the end we are left with a snooze button on all alarm clocks. Even my cell phone alarm has a snooze option. Seems odd: we have a product designed for a particular purpose and then create a button so that particular purpose doesn't function when it is supposed to.

Actually, I can appreciate this button. I have to admit that I have hit the snooze button more than a couple of times and have danced happily in that cosmic space that exists between being asleep and partially awake. I have actually set my alarm a couple minutes early so I could deactivate the alarm and ignore its original intent. To be completely honest, I have even been late for work before because I spent way too much time dabbling in no man's land. Nonetheless, I go on tapping the snooze button like I am playing the bongo drums.

Red Fox Fathers, I would guess that this is not the best book that you have ever read about fatherhood. If you are reading this, though, you care. You want to do better, and you are looking for insight. Nobody has all the answers for you; every child, situation, and father are different, and you aren't going to find all the answers by reading some book from some guy. Search your soul, listen to your heart, and listen to your kids. You will know the answer to meet your mission statement for your children.

I would ask that you consider this book your alarm. If you feel as if you are not engaged, not intentional, nor interactive, the alarm is sounding; it is time to get up. Now you can fold this book, set it on the counter, hit the snooze button and go back to your comfortable slumber of not being a Red Fox Father, or you can get up and be the kind of dad you wish you had when you were a little boy or be the father that saw this book and thought, "I need to change." You and I both know that it is late in the morning and your intention was to be a Red Fox Father by now. So go ahead, embrace your responsibilities, and start the new day; it is already too late for the snooze button, again.

So here is the challenge: what are you going to do differently? What are you going to take with you and place in your fatherhood arsenal? How are you going to change your outlook about being a father and not just a wage earner? To be good at anything, it takes a fair amount of planning; planning is strategy. Analyze, implement, adapt, analyze, implement, adapt, over and over again until you get it right. You can be That Dad.

Dad, don't hit the snooze; the alarm is blaring. Wake up, Dad, wake up. You may be late, but if you are alive to read this, then it's not too late.

Take it from the disappointed eight-year-old little boy who resides inside a formal living room on the green shag carpet in front of his parents as they sit on the orange-and-green paisley patterned couch telling me of their divorce.

"Dad, I want you to be part of my life. I need you to be a part of my life. I know it's not easy. I know you're busy, and I know that I can be difficult, but, remember, you only have me for fifteen minutes. Don't hit the snooze. We don't have much time"

Your child wants you and needs you to be That Dad.

Now it's time. The alarm sounds. Here we go for the last time, no snooze button to hit.

Be intentional, be engaged, be interactive. Be a Red Fox Father.

Now.

CPSIA information can be obtained at www.ICGtesting.com
Printed in the USA
LVOW081936200613

339468LV00002B/141/P

9 781462 727384